Jacqueline Kennedy Onassis

A TRIBUTE

Jacqueline Kennedy Onassis

A TRIBUTE

by Jacques Lowe

A
JACQUES LOWE
VISUAL ARTS PROJECTS
BOOK

JACQUES LOWE VISUAL ARTS PROJECTS NEW YORK

Contributors

A
JACQUES LOWE
VISUAL ARTS PROJECTS
BOOK

© 1995 Jacques Lowe

A Jacques Lowe Visual Arts Projects Book

Book design by Joseph Guglietti
Printed in Italy

Library of Congress Catalog Number:
CIP 95-078634
ISBN: 1-887767-00-2

Jacques Lowe Visual Arts Projects Inc.
138 Duane Street
New York, New York 10013

Foreword

Like the rest of the American public, the Leukemia Society was intensely saddened to learn in January, 1994, that Jacqueline Kennedy Onassis was stricken with non-Hodgkin's lymphoma. Although the Society has supported research that has improved survival rates to more than 53 percent, approximately 24,150 Americans will die of non-Hodgkin's lymphoma this year. Four short months after we learned of Mrs. Onassis' diagnosis, the disease took her.

As a result of this tragedy, the Society sought a way to honor her memory and intensify our efforts to defeat lymphoma. The Society established the *Jacqueline Kennedy Onassis Lymphoma Research Fund*. Not only will this support help us to discover the causes and eventual cures for lymphoma—we hope it will lead to the day when lymphoma is relegated to the history books.

One of Mrs. Onassis' wishes was to preserve her privacy and that of her children. Therefore we have chosen to remember her by presenting her most public moments as First Lady of the United States. With Jacques Lowe, Jacqueline and John F. Kennedy's personal photographer, the Society has created *A Tribute to Jackie: Jacques Lowe's Photo Exhibition to Benefit the Leukemia Society of America*. This beautiful exhibit has been specially designed by Mr. Lowe as a tribute to the woman who represented our country with grace, charm and dignity.

Every day the Leukemia Society of America is working diligently to find cures for leukemia, lymphoma, multiple myeloma and Hodgkin's disease. Until then, we are doing everything we can to improve quality of life for all patients and their families. Unfortunately, Mrs. Onassis could not be saved from the insidiousness of lymphoma. But, your support of the Society and the Jacqueline Kennedy Onassis Lymphoma Research Fund will help us accelerate cures for lymphoma and give new hope to the thousands who bravely battle the disease.

Your support is greatly appreciated.

Dwayne Howell

PRESIDENT & CEO
LEUKEMIA SOCIETY OF AMERICA

Artists imagine different worlds, better worlds. Jacqueline Kennedy Onassis encouraged all of us to do the same. As First Lady, Jackie Kennedy invited the great artists of the age to the White House for performances. She established a White House Fine Arts Committee, hired the first White House curator, and helped preserve such historic buildings as the Old Executive Office Building next to the White House. Her dream was to establish a federal Department of the Arts, which became realized in a slightly different version as the National Endowment for the Arts.

The writer Carl Anthony said, "She felt American culture was as good as European culture... most people have never fully appreciated how richly she contributed to the quality of American life in terms of bringing the arts and humanities to the American landscape." Her legacy is that she brought grace and imagination to her role, and she was instrumental in getting this country to realize the importance of culture and the arts to our daily lives. She believed in a better world.

Jane Alexander

MS. ALEXANDER IS CHAIRMAN OF THE NATIONAL ENDOWMENT OF THE ARTS

Jackie looked radiant that summer when JFK captured his party's presidential nomination. This is my favorite portrait of her. Although wearing a simple summer dress, devoid of jewelry or any other accouterments, she looks regal and serene, and astonishingly beautiful. She exudes inner strength and a certainty of purpose. No wonder many Americans admired and imitated her, and called her a queen.

8

HYANNIS PORT, MASSACHUSETTS. SUMMER 1960

Jackie…

J Jackie was really a very outstanding person. She had all of the tributes that a woman would like to be known for—she had beauty, she had charm, she had wit, she had understanding, and she was gracious. She was also very firm and would always stand up for what she believed in.

We lunched together quite often during the winter at a special table we had at Les Pleiades. It was off in the corner, so that we were away from most of the others. We would talk seriously, and, of course, we always laughed. That was one of the things that made Jackie so charming—she was so thoughtful and really so intellectual, but at the same time, she had the most delicious sense of humor.

I always looked forward to our meetings and would come away from them with my spirits uplifted. I would stand outside the door of the restaurant and look after her as she walked down the street on her way back to get one of her grandchildren to take to the park, either for a walk or a ride in the stroller.

Among her other qualities, she was a wonderful mother and was becoming a great grandmother. In any event, she will have left her mark in the world and in this country, people will always be proud of her.

Brooke Astor

MRS. ASTOR IS A NEW YORK-BASED AUTHOR AND PHILANTHROPIST

This family portrait was taken for the 1960 Christmas card. Jackie loved the picture, but wondered whether it was possible to replace Caroline's head with one from another frame which she preferred. I tried, but it was technically impossible. She finally decided to go ahead with this original.

HYANNIS PORT, MASSACHUSETTS. AUGUST 1960

I knew Jackie from the time we were both teenagers living in the Washington area. I was just ahead of her at Miss Porter's School in Farmington, Connecticut, and then at Vassar. When I started my first job at the American embassy in Paris, she arrived on the scene as a student at the Sorbonne. There was no way then to predict that within a decade she would be following the yellow brick road to the White House.

To meet her, even during her adolescent years, was never to forget her. She was a natural beauty—wearing none of the trappings of the teenage cosmetic fashions of the day. There were no globs of neon purple lipstick, no thick eyebrows blackened with strokes of a dark pencil. Nor did her skin suffocate under a thick layer of Pan-Cake makeup. Even more important to me in my earliest impression of this young girl was her voice—unforgettable in its soft, breathy tones. It was a sound that forced one to draw close and listen well.

She was born with a built-in fashion flair. So was her sister Lee Radziwill (it must have been in the Bouvier genes). That sense of style governed not only what she bought but the way she wore it. She frequently received letters from women who complained that they had purchased "exact copies" of the First Lady's outfits (usually mass-produced and in the marketplace six weeks after Jackie appeared in them), but "When I put on the dress, the effect isn't as dazzling." They simply could not understand why, if they were the same size, roughly the same age and clad in the same outfit, they did not look just like Jackie.

She received thousands of letters each week brimming with other questions. Nothing, it seemed, was too personal to ask: What is your diet? What do the children (and their animals!) eat? What brand of toothbrush do you use ("those wonderful teeth," they would exclaim in their letters)? And even, What laxative do you and the President take, because, as one correspondent concluded, "You look like regular people."

The letters I most liked to read were those that simply showed the writer's admiration for the First Lady and asked for nothing in return: "The happy, beautiful look on your children's faces shows what a good mother

This photograph was taken the first time I ever met Jack or Jackie Kennedy. We had earlier taken a formal portrait in the library that was to serve as a Christmas card, and I asked that we repeat a more relaxed group portrait on the porch. Caroline instinctively reached for her mother's pearls and put them in her mouth. The image, perhaps because of its innocence and simplicity, has become an icon.

HYANNIS PORT, MASSACHUSETTS. SUMMER 1958

you are" and "I tried putting some lilies of the valley in an antique porcelain mug in an unexpected corner of our living room, like I saw you had done in a photograph, and my husband and I look at it all the time. It's so beautiful—how wonderful you are to have things around you like that!"

Of course, they're gone now—the John F. Kennedys and their White House magic. The American public did not wish it to end, that allure and romance. But now there's a closure, and complaints are being heard throughout the land that people didn't know Jackie well enough during those White House years and after; even members of the younger generation who weren't around in the 1960s can't get enough of her today.

During the Kennedy administration Pam Turnure stood guarding her boss' privacy as Jackie's efficient press secretary; toward the end Nancy Tuckerman took over as White House social secretary, becoming the First Lady's lifelong and most trusted aide-de-camp. Whatever the world was able to learn about Jackie through her official duties and obvious devotion to her children, I don't think the public ever realized just how much she helped her husband behind the scenes.

Jackie would leave cartoons and limericks for Jack in unexpected places to cheer him up when the nation's affairs were going badly. She would arrange for special treats (like Joe's Stone Crabs from Miami and his favorite ice cream) to be served when he was under unusually great pressure in the Oval Office. With deft timing, old friends would pay morale-boosting calls at Jackie's prompting. But her most effective weapon in raising Jack's spirits was a surprise visit to his office with the children. And she labored more over his birthday celebrations than over any state dinner.

Many days she would be waiting by the elevator to the family apartment to help him when he emerged from it, dragging himself on crutches and in excruciating back pain. It was a sight the President would not have wanted outsiders to witness.

It's hard work being "First Lady," a title Jackie hated. Initially, she instructed her staff to refer to her as "Mrs. Kennedy," but that didn't last long. Tradition is a tough wrestling partner. Whether she was hosting an event for 2,000 people in ninety-degree heat in the backyard, as she once sarcastically described the South Lawn, or watching a cobra fight a mongoose to death (as Indian protocol dictated she do in Prime Minister Nehru's garden), she was ever the trooper.

People have never stopped talking about her manners. Jackie learned those as every young woman does—from her mother, as a little girl. Her handwritten notes were beautiful—not only in their warm, affectionate style but in their frequency and timing. The morning after a dinner, the day after a bouquet was received, out a note would go, with its simply engraved "The White House" heading the stationery.

Sometimes in those notes—and virtually everywhere else—there would be glimpses of her humor. She sought the fun in any situation and seemed to have a continually amused sparkle in her eye—even if always holding others at a distance. Washington saw much mimicking and limerick spouting at parties during the Kennedy years. The popular French ambassador, Hervè Alphand, for example, was famous for performing his imitations of world leaders as after-dinner entertainment at the French embassy. Jackie is the only person I have known who could imitate Ambassador Alphand imitating President Charles de Gaulle. (Even Robin Williams would have a hard time doing that.)

Witty, bright, generous of spirit: Those enduring qualities form a mental scrapbook of endless pages. But as the future begins to slip by even more quickly than the past, what will my overriding memory of Jackie be? As the regal chatelaine of the Number One House of the land (make that the *world*)? When somebody dies, one tends to remember a definitive image of that person. Mine will certainly *not* be the one television gave us of her coffin about to be lowered into the earth at Arlington National Cemetery—a casket shining so cleanly and peacefully in the sun, decorated so tastefully with greenery on the top, centered with a simple white cross of flowers.

No, my image through the years ahead will be of her in the white silk Givenchy ball gown she wore during a 1961 state visit to France for the farewell dinner President and Madame de Gaulle hosted in the Hall of Mirrors in Versailles. The top of her white dress was a veritable painting of pastel flowers, all hand-embroidered in paillettes. The President was unbelievably handsome that night in his white tie and tails. Jackie and Jack looked at one another with open admiration as they left Paris arm in arm for Versailles. They were, after all, a team, and this balmy June evening was a far cry from the campaign trail back home. The air around them was literally charged with electricity from the synergy of their presence, physical appearance, talent and youth. The de Gaulles and every other guest at that large formal dinner were transfixed by the two of them all evening long.

We watched a ballet commissioned by Louis XV himself. It was more than magical. It was a dream sequence for every member of the White House party fortunate enough to be present. No one enjoyed or appreciated it more than John and Jacqueline Kennedy.

When the evening was over and the single file of limousines wound its way back to Paris through the beautifully lit gardens and *allèes* of trees in the Parc de Versailles, we suddenly heard the American and then the French national anthems over loudspeakers. The Kennedys stopped the procession and got out of their car. No one would have dared follow them. They walked alone to a giant, illuminated fountain as the music continued playing through the trees. They stood hand in hand in silence, savoring this moment in history for at least five minutes, their figures silhouetted against the fountain's dancing, flickering waters. I was not the only one to hold my breath.

That is the image I will always take with me: of the two of them, the Presidential team, hand in hand, giving a premier performance on a state visit to a foreign land, doing us proud.

Utter perfection. Taste and grace.

Jackie in Caroline's nursery at the Kennedy's Georgetown town-house at 3307 N Street.

Letitia Baldridge

MRS. BALDRIDGE WAS JACQUELINE KENNEDY'S SOCIAL SECRETARY IN THE KENNEDY WHITE HOUSE

GEORGETOWN, SPRING 1959

W

Whenever I think back on it, as I am now forced to do, it is with utter dread and horror. It was late in the afternoon of a very full day in the Sixties. I stumbled into the receiving line, made up of four lovely ladies, self-evidently the sponsors of the charity affair.

The first in line was my wife, the other three all very familiar faces—no doubt I had been in their company dozens of times. But in that harassed moment I could not instantly remember their names, so I did what one generally does in those situations. After kissing my own wife, I went on to buss Lady B (whom indeed I did know), then Lady C (whom indeed I did know), then Jackie Kennedy—whom I had never laid eyes on in my life.

It was only after I had treated her like one of my old lady-buddies that recognition set in. I felt exactly as I'd have felt if I had accidentally kissed the Queen of England. Not because Jackie was Untouchable; but because the national mania to touch her made her correspondingly vulnerable. For a while, a long while, I felt like that awful paparazzo she finally took to court because he was following her about with his camera day after day, month after month.

In the years ahead, we became moderate friends, and once during a fire drill at Doubleday I shared a concrete stair with her for the duration. Our contacts were infrequent, and I rather liked that about her. She had a set of friends, and as the years went by, she gave more time to consolidating friendships that especially appealed to her than to quick-processing fresh friends. If it had happened that, a month ago, we had been seated together, whether in a staircase during a fire drill or at a fancy party, the conversation would have been fresh and lively and spontaneous, utterly lacking in strain; in part, I must suppose, because she knew that notwithstanding the first awful misadventure, I was not engaged in cultivating Jacqueline Kennedy Onassis.

I did once ask her to engage in an enterprise that would have required her to spend ten minutes at the Sistine Chapel, reflecting on the continuing relevance of one of the parables in the New Testament. Her negative was

Senator Kennedy, Jackie and Caroline pose for a portrait in their N Street townhouse. That portrait was the first cover assignment I had from a major magazine. Kennedy still was one of seven unannounced presidential candidates. The contest had not yet begun in earnest.

GEORGETOWN. FALL 1959

charmingly delivered over the telephone. "Bill, the only time I ever appeared on television was when I took the camera around the White House after the renovations. I was so awful I decided never to do it again."

It seems, on reflection, that her life, for all its vicissitudes, was about as perfectly conducted as anyone with her beauty, skills and glamour could hope to manage. She did what she wanted to do. If her second marriage was emotionally impulsive, it was strategically prudent. Books could be written (probably have been written) on the skills she showed in bringing up her two exemplary children in that magnetic field she moved in. She worked not as a dilettante but as a truly engaged editor, an average of three days every week. She exhibited only as much of herself as she thought she owed as reciprocity to a country that loved her and was fascinated by her.

And she was true to her Christian faith, which in the final ceremony irradiated Jackie's class, a creature of God.

William F. Buckley

MR. BUCKLEY IS EDITOR-IN-CHIEF OF *NATIONAL REVIEW*

Senator Kennedy interrupts a meeting with his brother-in-law Steve Smith and his executive assistant and speech writer Theodore "Ted" Sorensen to join Jackie and Caroline in the backyard of their home on N Street.

GEORGETOWN. SPRING 1959

21

When she arrived at the White House, she had no clothes. For about 10 days, she wouldn't go out. The popular idea is that Jackie arrived with hundreds of dresses. The reality was that she was a photographic reporter and she'd lived with controlled simplicity. The moment she was in the White House, she was another person. She was suddenly confronted with so many things to do, and she had to play the part.

She wanted a look, not attractive dresses. I was called by her secretary and given three days to present a wardrobe. She was in the hospital at the time, having just given birth to John. I created her look. She asked me, "How do you see me in my role?" I presented her with a philosophy of quiet, sober elegance. Everyone copied her.

Later, Jackie called me from France and asked, "Should I have a dress made by a French designer to make the French happy?" She was very proud and very happy with her wardrobe. She asked me if I would mind if she had one Givenchy dress. I said, "It's perfectly beautiful that you bothered to ask me."

I always considered her to be an Egyptian princess. She had an architectural look—wonderful shoulders, a long waist, the kind of figure that would carry a dress.

Oleg Cassini

MR. CASSINI IS A NEW YORK-BASED FASHION DESIGNER

Jackie poses with Caroline on the sun porch in Hyannis Port for some international magazine covers.

GEORGETOWN. SPRING 1959

23

I In the old days, when I worked with Andy Warhol—a certain stretch in the seventies—he went to Jackie's Christmas party every year. In 1979, Andy said we should go. I said, "She knows me. If she wanted an editor from *Interview*, and if she wanted to invite me, she would have." But you can always bring one person to a cocktail party. Which journalist, which American wouldn't want to see the inside of Jackie O's apartment? She greeted us at the door and she couldn't have been nicer. She introduced me to Peter Duchin and Arthur Schlesinger, Jr. and asked me what I'd like to drink. I said Perrier, and she had just run out, so she gave me hers. She asked some people to stay for dinner—Andy and me too. It was a simple but perfect buffet, ham and turkey. I was so happy! So, the next morning she calls Andy on the dot of nine, and as Andy put it, "gave [him] a piece of her mind" for inviting a gossip columnist.

Bob Colacello

MR. COLACELLO IS A NEW YORK-BASED WRITER

The small antique secretaire in the living room of their home served as Jackie's office, where she answered mail and sent and received invitations.

GEORGETOWN. FALL 1959

J Jacqueline Kennedy Onassis was my editor. Even now it sounds pretentious to say it, and over the years I worked with her I never quite got used to the fact.

She purchased my first manuscript on behalf of Doubleday after fifteen editors at other publishing houses had rejected it. I was expecting a rejection letter through my agent when she called me personally to say she liked the manuscript and wanted to acquire it.

I often found people more interested in the fact that she was editing my book than in the fact that I was writing it. I remember moments of feeling disgruntled, as if she had stolen my show. I began to stammer when people asked who my editor was, wanting to say, and not wanting to say, and not knowing whether to call her Jacqueline Kennedy Onassis or Jackie Onassis or Mrs. Onassis. She never gave me any clues about such things and I never dared to ask, knowing it would be a reference to the fact that she was famous: a fact that neither of us ever referred to, as it was far too personal.

It seemed, in the beginning, that she trusted me before I had earned it. I became skittish. Not knowing what, if anything, I had done to deserve her trust, I feared what I might do by accident to lose it. Not that she confided private thoughts to me. Rather, she trusted me not to ask about them. I never did. I felt that in a small, implicit way I had been enlisted as another guardian of Camelot.

Oddly enough it was her shyness that put me at ease. I only met with her a few times in person; most of our work was done through correspondence and over the telephone. But she was very much a working editor. I have kept most of her written editorial comments, stuffing them too carelessly in a disorderly file marked "Doubleday." Looking through them now I see the ways she shaped my stories.

She knew where drama was, and where it wasn't. I see the words "CUT" and "DELETE" many times, written in capitals and underlined for emphasis. Page 334: "Cut baby crying." Page 345: "Cut chickens." Page 364:

GEORGETOWN, SPRING 1959

"Overkill. Can you delete?" On page 101 of one rough draft she has written, "Much of Kate and William's relationship is cloying. You must eliminate some of her angst, their coy dialogues, her hemming and hawing, etc." And pages later, "Too much Coon Dog. Too much Crucita. Don't let yourself go overboard with Coon Dog. There is too much about the stump of his tail." She was always as attuned to what should be left out as to what should be put in. "De la Rosa—one could fall in love with him. But when you overdo describing him, it undercuts his power, makes him sound out of Central Casting." And "Baby Samuel is so overdescribed it could turn one off babies."

A brief moment of intimacy as Senator Kennedy pauses in the hallway before leaving for Capitol Hill.

It is the affirmations, not the strictures, though, that I remember best. "You must be glowing," she wrote in reference to one particularly good review. "I have never seen anything so superlative in my life." In one hand-written letter I will always treasure, she wrote, "I am so impressed by what you have done, I just can't tell you. You have pared down and tightened a sprawling overwritten first draft into an immensely moving novel…Bravo and with affection, Jackie."

She was motherly, that way. So warm and personal in a professional relationship, that I often felt uncertain how I should respond. We were comrades, not friends. I knew nothing of her private life, though she sometimes signed her letters, "Love, Jackie," which both touched and disconcerted me, placing me in the quandary of how I should sign mine to her.

Yet with all her kindness, she had no tolerance for sap. "Don't allow yourself to be repetitious or sentimental," she wrote in reference to an early draft. "It backfires." Page 56: "Melodrama; I'd eliminate." Page 308: "This is pretty trite. Can you recast?" Page 600: "Overwritten, overwrought."

She cared that every sentence be correct in language, in emotion, and in detail. Page 192: "Eliminate 'with' and put a comma after 'doorway.' You do this often—incorrectly use 'with' as a connective to cobble together two disparate thoughts." Page 643: " 'hocking mucus.' This is the third or fourth time you have used this image. The reader gets irritated." Page 857: " 'Gaucho hat.' Gaucho is Argentinean. Would that term have been used here?"

GEORGETOWN, SPRING 1959

In the beginning, I asked if she would prefer to see each chapter as I wrote it, or several at a time. She chose the latter. "But if you need some hand holding through the forest," she wrote, "you must do whatever makes you feel best."

She sent me the first copy of my second novel at about the time she was diagnosed. Right up to the month before she died, she continued to champion the book at Doubleday, pressing the editor-in-chief for more promotion funds. In my last communication from her, in the midst of all the turmoil that goes with publication of a book, she wrote, "Stay calm! You have a winner."

There were times I disagreed with her suggestions. She wasn't always right. But she sustained my effort and her editing improved my books in ways impossible to measure. To use a childish image, which she likely would have labeled maudlin and affected, and which in fact is, but to use it anyway because it keeps returning to me in a vivid way, I see her as a fairy godmother. She appeared at a difficult time and gave me what I wanted most—to see my books in print. Then she disappeared.

Riding piggy-back was one of Caroline's favorite games.

Elizabeth Crook

MS. CROOK AUTHORED SEVERAL BOOKS EDITED BY JACQUELINE KENNEDY ONASSIS

HYANNIS PORT, MASSACHUSETTS. SUMMER 1961

J Jackie Onassis was my friend.

I don't know any better way to put it. She was also my editor. I worked on two books with Jackie, one abut a single mother and social worker from Portsmouth named Dorothy Redford and the other about a former Alabama congressman named Carl Elliot.

Jackie made both those books happen. She was a matchmaker and a midwife. That's what she did for Doubleday in New York, the publisher for which she worked until the day she died—she made books happen, scanning the landscape for stories, bringing subjects and writers together to put those stories on the page, then doing whatever it took to usher them through that process.

It was her innate, sincere curiosity that came through the first time we talked, after I had signed with Doubleday to write the book on Dorothy and Jackie called to congratulate me and to introduce herself, to say how excited she was that we'd be working together.

She actually *sounded* excited and her voice was nothing like the soft, wispy one the nation heard when she took us through the White House back in the early 1960s. The voice I heard in that first conversation and in all our talks that followed was huskier, with a New York tint to it—Brooklyn, almost—and it was alive, effusive, almost girlish in its enthusiasm.

It was that earnest enthusiasm, not just for books but for people, that struck me most about Jackie. She dealt with dozens, maybe hundreds of writers, but whenever I left a message, she always called back, right away. Sometimes my daughter Jamie picked up the phone, and Jackie would keep her on the line for a minute or two, like a relative. Like a friend. Then Jamie would pass the phone to me, whispering, "It's President Kennedy's old wife."

That's what Jackie was to Jamie, and to most of America. Larger than life. The Queen of Camelot. But to me she was an encouraging colleague, which I often needed, especially during the dark winter I spent in the coal country of north Alabama, working on the Carl Elliott book.

The peaceful, idyllic, almost poetic scene in Hyannis Port soon gave way to more frantic commotion as the general election campaign got on its way.

HYANNIS PORT, MASSACHUSETTS. SUMMER 1960

Jackie cared about Carl. She called often just to see how he was doing, this old friend of Jack Kennedy's, this Alabama liberal who was now in his 70s, living out a life ruined by the stand he took against the evil wave that was George Wallace. Jackie had been there when Carl Elliott went down in the early '60s, and she was there now, 30 years later, calling every couple of weeks to see how Carl was feeling, if his diabetes was letting him have a good day or not.

She'd mention the book we were writing, but that wasn't what mattered most. Even when we talked, Jackie and I, that wasn't what mattered most. She always wanted to know how I was doing, and I became comfortable enough to tell her. At my lowest point when the book was stalled, when the winter was at its bleakest and a long separation from my wife was finally becoming a divorce, Jackie and I had some of our most extended conversations. She knew better than to offer advice. But she made sure that I knew she was there, anytime. Just pick up the phone, she told me. And when I had to, I did.

I knew nothing about her personal life, didn't ask, wasn't interested. We had a relationship of our own, something real, something I valued, and that was enough. I never went up to New York to see her, never did lunch, though she invited me. Maybe I didn't want even a hint of schmoozing, of trading on her fame. I didn't need to go to New York. Certainly not for lunch.

The only time I ever asked her about herself was the last time we talked. I had called with a quick question, and as usual, Jackie called right back. We took care of business, then I asked how she was feeling. Her cancer was headline news by then. Wonderful, she told me. She was feeling wonderful. She was due for a checkup, some sort of procedure in June, and she was doing great.

And now this. Wire reports. Television specials. Phone calls from people who know I knew her, all asking me what I can tell them about Jackie.

Not much, I guess. I never met her.

But she was my friend.

Mike D'Orso

MR. D'ORSO IS A WRITER LIVING IN NORFOLK, VIRGINIA

The Kennedys in the senator's office on Capitol Hill. Jackie often assisted her husband dealing mainly with French and Spanish constituents' questions.

WASHINGTON, D.C. FALL 1958

O Of course, she always seemed remote, aloof, private in the extreme, and unattainable, yet people, even people who had never met her, called her Jackie when they talked about her, because she was a part of the personal history of every American who was alive on that terrible day 30 years ago, recalled each time someone asks, "Do you remember where you were on the day President Kennedy was shot?" That day her image became engraved on our souls. If she enjoyed privilege, her privilege was never resented, because she had earned it with her courage. In New York, she could be seen doing the things that all New Yorkers do—hailing cabs, going to work, walking in Central Park, taking in a movie on Lexington Avenue. Apart from the pesky paparazzi, people did not intrude on her privacy, except maybe to call out, "Hi, Jackie" when they passed her, and some of them received a smile back, or a wave, as she kept on walking her fast walk, with her eyes raised just high enough to avoid eye contact, in the celebrity manner of seeing but not seeing called blindsight. Once, I saw her standing on a long line for the ladies' room at Radio City Music Hall during an intermission at Francis Ford Coppala's reissue of Abel Gance's great film, *Napoleon*. I can think of a whole list of people far less famous than she who would have found a way to get to the head of that line.

The public easily tires of icons, but America's fascination with Jacqueline Bouvier Kennedy Onassis never burned out; it remained as constant as the eternal flame she designated for her husband's grave. Her fame was free of the resentment that fame sometimes produces, because she didn't work at it, and she never grabbed for the perks that accompany it. No publicists plotted her course. No perfume company paid for her name to advertise its product. She was simply who she was, part of the fabric of American culture. In grand circles, the word "class" is considered a bad–taste word, but class is really the key word to describe her. Style, chic, and other such attributes are acquirable; class is not. Either you have it or you don't. Jackie had it in spades.

The news of her death, though not unexpected, still stunned when it came. The immediate feeling was different from that experienced at a

This mini Merry-Go-Round, recently installed on the lawn of the Kennedy compound, served as a center of amusement for all the Kennedy children present— Caroline, Bobby Kennedy's eight children, Stevie Smith, Maria and Bobby Shriver, and all their friends. The place absolutely teemed with children, their pets, their nurses and their toys.

HYANNIS PORT, MASSACHUSETTS. SUMMER 1960

hearing of the death of a world-famous woman—Golda Meir, Indira Gandhi, Eleanor Roosevelt, for instance, all of whom were revered. The feeling was more personal. Yes, there was grief, and there was sorrow. But mostly there was loss. Someone the country cherished was gone, and it seemed quite likely that the void she left in our lives could never be filled.

She had belonged to us for more than 30 years. We had watched her react and then act with magnificence at the most horrible moment of her life, and we would never forget it. With the instinctive knowledge of the great, knowing when their moment is at hand, she in effect picked up the flag dropped by her fallen husband and did what no one would have expected of her in the immediate shock of his violent death. She remained at Parkland Memorial Hospital until the doctors pronounced him dead. She refused to change her bloodstained pink suit. She stood by Lyndon Johnson in the plane as he took the oath of office. She was only 34 years old, more or less the same age as her children at the time of her death.

She had a sense of history. It was she who asked to have the details of Abraham Lincoln's funeral studied in order to give her husband the sort of state funeral she wanted for him. From that Lincoln research came the riderless horse with the boots turned backward. Through television, the Kennedy funeral was the first great historical media event in which the whole world participated. For four days she defined nobility of behavior, teaching us how to mourn with dignity. Sadly, that nobility of behavior has subsequently slipped out of our lives.

After the assassination of Robert Kennedy, with whom she had become close after the president's assassination, she feared for the safety of her Kennedy children. "I don't want my children to live here anymore. If they're killing Kennedys, my kids are number-one targets. . . I want to get out of this country," she said at the time.

She was far too young for the life of perpetual widowhood and sainthood that the public demanded of her. She went through a period of disfavor when she married Aristotle Onassis, an unattractive but engaging and immensely rich man, more notorious than famous, whose penchant for gross extravagance and unfortunate public behavior sullied and stained her goddesslike stature for the few years they were together. She was portrayed as money-mad, jewelry-mad, a world-class shopper. Even her most devoted friends were aghast at her choice, and acknowledge that the marriage was a mistake.

Following her second widowhood, she did not retreat into the social life of New York that was so available to her and that so longed for her presence. She did not become a fixture on the party circuit. On the rare occasion— several times a year—when she appeared at social functions, she always caused a hush when she entered a room. Even the most sophisticated people turned and stared at her. No one was ever so used to her that her arrival or departure went unnoticed. She stood for the requisite moments of picture taking, always understanding the exigencies of fame. When she moved in, the crowd gave way for her. She was what royals used to be but so seldom are any longer. People never rushed up to talk to her. She would recognize a face and speak to that person. In conversation, her eyes rarely wandered from the eye of the person to whom she was speaking.

Everyone who ever came in contact with her has a story to tell. Glenn Bernbaum, the proprietor of Mortimer's, the tony Upper East Side restaurant where Jackie often met friends and authors for lunch, told me of the time Claudette Colbert, the famed film star now in her 90s, stopped to speak to him as she was leaving the restaurant. When she was outside, Jackie went up to Bernbaum and asked, almost in awe, "Was that Claudette Colbert?" Upon learning that it was, Jackie followed her out onto the street, introduced herself, and engaged her in conversation. Elaine Kaufman, the proprietor of Elaine's, the popular watering hole for the literary set, where Jackie sometimes dined with her writer pals, told me that she always placed her at a table near the back, where she could have privacy but still observe the action of the sometimes boisterous clientele. In recent years, Jackie would occasionally call and say that her son, John, was coming that evening with a group of his friends, and that Elaine should send the bill to her.

She became a respected editor, first at Viking and later at Doubleday. Authors of hers I talked to told me how astonished they were at her ease in dealing with them. When the receptionist would call to say that a writer was waiting in the lobby, Jackie would come out to greet him and lead him back to her office, and later would walk him out to the elevator. She was meticulous and thorough in her editorial notes on manuscripts. Stephen Rubin, the president and publisher of Doubleday, said, "She had an uncanny knack for picking great projects and a delight in bringing them to fruition. But that only scratched the surface of her here. She was caring and loving and perceptive with her co-workers. She had an extraordinary relationship with the staff, who are devastated by her death."

The only time I ever actually had a conversation with her was at a lunch party at Mortimer's to celebrate the publication of a book she had edited about Fred Astaire, a compilation of pictures and quotes about the great star from friends and co-workers whom my friend Sarah Giles had interviewed. I had always longed to meet her, but when the moment came, I couldn't think of a single thing to say. "Oh, God, don't let me go mute," I prayed. The slight smile on her face indicated that she knew that people sometimes had that feeling in her presence. Of course, she saved the day. She mentioned a quote of mine in the book and asked me something about Fred Astaire, whom I had known because his daughter was a friend of mine, and suddenly I was off and running. Only later did I realize that I had done all the talking. She had just given me the subject.

On occasion she put her fame to good use, as in her fight to preserve Grand Central Terminal when the venerable New York landmark was threatened with having a skyscraper built over it. She took a train to Washington with other members of the committee, and her magical presence did much to save the stately structure built by the Vanderbilts in 1913. In the days following her death, a long table with two large guest books and a huge bouquet of flowers was set up in a restored waiting room in Grand Central so that people could respectfully sign their names or leave a note for her children. Inscribed on a seven-foot aluminum plaque under a spotlight was the inscription "Jacqueline Kennedy Onassis led the fight to save this beautiful terminal. The victory won in the United States Supreme Court in 1978 established the public's right to protect landmarks in cities and towns all over America."

She considered Caroline and John to be the great accomplishments of her life, and they have responded by becoming ideals for the young of their

During that lovely late summer of 1960 the Kennedy compound was overrun by countless children and other people's pets. Here she enjoys a private moment with her Caroline and her own pet.

40

HYANNIS PORT, MASSACHUSETTS. SPRING 1960

generation at a time when so many young people have slipped into drugs and decadence. Each has grown up to represent a different side of their mother: Caroline has her mother's strength, intelligence, and sense of privacy; John has inherited her star quality and her ability to dazzle in public life. The moment she whispered to three-year-old John to salute his father as the casket rolled by, she thrust fame upon him. We have watched that child grow up to be one of the most romantic figures in the world, based as yet largely on his looks and heritage. We know, however, that he was never spoiled. He has never grabbed a paparazzo's camera and smashed it, although there have been times in his life when he had a right to. When he walked out of his mother's building on the night of her death and announced to the media that she was gone, his authority was consummate. When he spoke at her grave in Arlington, he exhibited the natural ease of his father.

Jacqueline Kennedy Onassis gave only two personal interviews after her husband's assassination, to Theodore White and William Manchester, and both of them were sealed: White's was not to be opened until a year after her death, Manchester's until the year 2067. But think what she must have experienced. Think what she died knowing. Perhaps to her intimates—Caroline, John, Maurice Tempelsman—she has told her story, knowing that she could trust them totally, that they would never betray her wishes. Perhaps, one day, they will share with us those parts of her story that she wanted to give to her public.

Jackie and Caroline in Caroline's nursery. Jackie was telling her a story about what different people do in a city.

Dominick Dunne

MR. DUNNE IS AN AUTHOR AND FREQUENT CONTRIBUTOR TO *VANITY FAIR*

GEORGETOWN SPRING 1959

43

Jacqueline Bouvier Kennedy Onassis was the most private public person on earth. She gave only one interview in person in the last thirty years—to a publishing trade journal, and only on the condition that it would focus on her work as a book editor. The last interview before that was in 1963 with Theodore H. White for *Life* magazine, in which she immortalized John F. Kennedy's fabled Presidency as Camelot. After her husband's assassination, she sat for only one portrait and never once posed for a formal photograph—which only made the paparazzi stalk her with a greater vengeance and kept the tabloids and other vultures at the ready.

Blue-blooded debutante, First Lady, Fata Morgana, tragic heroine, rich man's prized possession, impassioned preservationist. The perceptions of her—and the truth—are many. But as far as she was concerned she was, first and last, a mother. On more than one occasion, she said that she felt her finest accomplishment, hands down, was raising two relatively normal children under highly unusual circumstances. That was putting it mildly.

Her marriage to Aristotle Onassis tested the loyalty of her fans, gave grudging admirers the perfect excuse to sling some mud and became a field day for the press. How could she? Why would she? What's he got—besides more money than Zeus? She suffered the censure and went on with her life, with no apologies.

To go from calling her Jacqueline Kennedy to Jackie Onassis and then Jackie O. was a big adjustment for Americans. Many still haven't made it: "She will always be Mrs. Kennedy to me," they will say.

It was Mrs. Kennedy, after all, who lost two children she wanted badly (a stillborn daughter in 1956 and a two-day-old son in 1963), the husband she loved, and the brother-in-law she had come to depend on for solace. She grieved, but not in public. When her husband was assassinated before her eyes and the world's, she rose above her own needs and got us through four of the darkest days in our history by thinking first of others—in this case, the American people. Perhaps she thought, "I'll have the rest of my life to mourn." Whatever propelled her, kept her moving forward, head high and eyes dry but for a single tear, she became the role model for every widow who ever was to be.

On election day morning: shortly after returning from exercising their vote in Hyannis Port, the Kennedys posed for me on the lawn of their summer house. JFK was not yet the president, but there was no doubt in his mind that he would be elected. It would take a long day and an anxious night and morning, with his lead diminishing from two million at midnight to barely 100,000 before he would finally be elected.

44

HYANNIS PORT, MASSACHUSETTS, NOVEMBER 1960

45

Later, to be constantly reminded that her red-blooded husband had been so outrageously unfaithful so close to home must have been torture. To have books, movies, TV dramatizations, talk shows, silent stares and strobe lights coming every which way could not have made for an easy transition into private life. But, amazingly, she managed to live in relative quiet, dividing her time among her apartment on upper Fifth Avenue, a house on Martha's Vineyard, a farm in Bernardsville, New Jersey, and a cottage in Middleburg, Virginia. She even found a trusted companion in Maurice Templesman, a financier and longtime adviser.

In addition to her unpaid efforts to preserve Grand Central Terminal and other landmarks, she had a fulfilling career as a book editor. It was in that capacity that I and three of my *Town & Country* colleagues met with her. Doubleday had called, inquiring if we might be interested in excerpting material from a book on Toni Frissell, a society and fashion photographer. Mrs. Onassis had taken on this project with great zest not only because Frissell had photographed the Bouvier-Kennedy wedding in 1953 but more because she believed Frissell had been a great photographer whose work deserved to be published.

We liked what we saw so much that we decided to run the photographs in our upcoming October issue, to coincide with the publication of the book. Upon hearing that, Mrs. Onassis invited us to come by her office in order to look at the original material and then discuss our plans. There wasn't a chance-in-a-million that we wouldn't have accepted the invitation.

Our appointment was for April 5, just weeks, as it turned out, after the announcement that Mrs. Onassis had non-Hodgkin's lymphoma. Naturally, we were prepared for the meeting to be canceled. No such thing. On that day, I arrived and gave my name to the receptionist. Out of the corner of my eye, I could see a familiar figure walking toward the desk. "Emma," the little-girl's voice said, "I'm starving. Do you have any of those candies you keep?" Emma produced a handful. Mrs. Onassis then turned to me and said, with the sweetest smile, "Would you like a Tootsie Roll?" That is how we met.

She led me to the conference room, talking all the way, asking questions about the magazine and referring to stories she'd read in this issue or that. We joined a small group of people—no more than five—excitedly poring

During that relative quiet period in the Kennedy's life before Senator Kennedy declared his run for the presidency, Jackie was able to devote much time to her daughter, to decorating the house, and to entertaining.

GEORGETOWN. SPRING 1959

47

over the photographs. What I recall most vividly about the meeting was how happy Mrs. Onassis was that we were excerpting the book. It was as if it were her personal mission to see that Toni Frissell received her due.

She was simply dressed—a tailored jacket over a plain sweater and slacks. The only telling signs that anything was wrong were a bandage on her cheek and what was clearly a wig. There were certainly no other hints of any sort that she was not well—in fact, she was downright bubbly. At one point, she remembered something she'd wanted us to see, dashed out of the room and came back with a children's book and a folder full of photos. I was sitting in a chair and she plopped—yes, plopped—on the floor next to me and began showing and telling, with the enthusiasm of a seven-year-old. As she did, she would point to something and look me in the eyes. I prayed she wouldn't look too closely because she would have seen that my own eyes had welled up. Here was the world's most famous woman sitting on the floor beside me, hoping I would be interested in what she was showing me. We left, my colleagues and I, moved mightily by the experience.

The day after Mrs. Onassis died, we decided to slow down the presses on our July issue in order to create a special tribute. I knew it would be at tremendous cost and an inconvenience to everyone's schedule. No one seemed to mind in the least, including all those friends, acquaintances, writers and photographers we called upon to help us create this tribute (and to whom I give my thanks). On the contrary, it seemed fitting to put the former First Lady first.

More than any other woman who ever lived, Jacqueline Bouvier Kennedy Onassis embodied everything *Town & Country* stands for—love of family, devotion to one's country, loyalty to friends, grace, good manners, glamour, elegance, kindness and courage.

Now she is dead—as if everything she endured weren't enough to earn her a long life. On the other hand, maybe it means she gets to heaven, where she belongs, that much sooner. May she finally find her peace.

Pamela Fiori

MS. FIORI IS EDITOR-IN-CHIEF OF *TOWN & COUNTRY MAGAZINE*

Senator Kennedy, with Jackie, his aide Dave Powers, accompanied by Congresswoman Edith Green of that state, arrives at dusk for a political appearance. Only three supporters came to meet him. It became the future president's favorite picture. "Nobody remembers that today," he exclaimed later, alluding to the fact that they were ignored.

PORTLAND, OREGON. FALL 1959

49

It is an honor to have been asked to serve as an Honorary Chair for *A Tribute to Jackie*. As a former First Lady, I have long admired her charm and individuality. As a survivor of breast cancer, I know the fear that comes with the word cancer. Jackie's own battle was valiant and showed us once again her great strength and grace during a very stressful period. There is never enough money to do all the research needed to find the cure for cancer. I am especially pleased to be paying tribute to Jackie through an effort that will benefit the Jacqueline Kennedy Onassis Lymphoma Research Fund.

As a young Congressional wife, I was aware of the pretty young photographer who was about to become the bride of the Senator from Massachusetts. Jack Kennedy and Jerry Ford had offices across the hall from each other when they were both serving in the House and remained good friends. Like so many others, we enjoyed being part of the years the Kennedys spent in Washington.

As First Lady, Jacqueline Kennedy Onassis served with an abundance of grace and style. She will be held in our highest regard for years to come. Thank you for allowing me to be part of this tribute.

En route to California from West Virginia, Jackie relaxes with Jack Kerouac's famous book about the Beat Generation, "On The Road."

Betty Ford

MRS. FORD IS A FORMER FIRST LADY OF THE UNITED STATES AND
HONORARY CHAIR OF "A TRIBUTE TO JACKIE"

ABOARD THE CAROLINE, KENNEDY'S PRIVATE PLANE. SPRING 1960

I first met Jackie Onassis in the mid-1970s through her great interest in The Costume Institute at the Metropolitan Museum.

We had taken on Diana Vreeland as a consultant in 1972 to help organize major costume exhibitions and bring this area alive for the public. Jackie had been friends with Mrs. Vreeland for a long time, and was very supportive of her efforts at the museum.

Jackie became seriously involved with "The Glory of the Russian Costume" in 1976. She had traveled to Russia with the then-director, Thomas Hoving, and Vreeland when the initial choices were being made for the show.

There was quite a stir in Moscow and St. Petersburg when the widow of President Kennedy appeared in the Office of the Minister of Culture or at the Hermitage. The usual bureaucratic barriers, delays and obstacles to borrowing sensitive pre-revolutionary material were greatly reduced.

This was a beautiful and popular exhibition which opened people's eyes to aspects of an extraordinarily vibrant culture that had been suppressed since the Russian Revolution. Jackie edited the handsome and scholarly catalog, which was broadly distributed and gave a new importance to the Costume Institute and its publications.

Of great interest was Jackie's delightful and spirited essay, "A Visit to the High Priestess of Vanity Fair," in a small publication for the Museum's "Vanity Fair" exhibition in 1977. Her interview with Diana Vreeland brought the Vreeland style, curiosity and fabulous imagination to life in a remarkable way.

In the following years when I knew Jackie much better, she told me a story about the museum that I don't think has ever been published.

In 1963, Egyptian President Nasser offered the United States its choice of one of the monuments from Egypt which had been rescued from the rising waters of Lake Nasser.

One Sunday evening after dinner, President Kennedy handed her a notebook with photographs of 12 Egyptian monuments from Nubia. Jackie

CALIFORNIA. FALL 1959

53

looked through the photographs; the one that appealed to her immediately was the Temple of Dendur, standing on the bank of the Nile between Aswan and Abu Simbel.

That was the one she chose. The government of Egypt subsequently gave the temple to the United States, which initially awarded it to the Smithsonian to be placed in the open air along the Potomac River.

Brooke Astor, a trustee of the Metropolitan, interceded with Lady Bird Johnson, and an architectural competition was held to give other institutions a chance. The Metropolitan won, and placed the temple in a beautiful glass-enclosed space allowing it to be seen from outside the museum.

Jackie said that she always loved the temple because she could look out and see it from her Fifth Avenue apartment, especially at night when it is dramatically lit.

Jackie was very supportive when Phillippe de Montebello established the museum's Office of Film and Television, headed by Karl Katz. Beginning in 1980, the museum produced more than 35 films for television relating to our exhibitions and permanent collections. Especially in the early years, Jackie was instrumental in getting corporate, foundation and private support for this new educational enterprise—reaching a greatly expanded audience.

Another interest I shared with her was the preservation of great architecture. We were both members of the Board of the Municipal Art Society.

There were many people who felt close to this extraordinary woman; she had a remarkable gift for friendship, a wonderful sense of humor, and a great love of art and beauty. She once said about Grand Central Terminal, which she was instrumental in saving, "If we don't care about our past, we cannot hope for the future."

She always hoped for the future and helped a lot of others do the same.

The role of political wives during the fifties and sixties was to sit by and wait while their husbands made their speeches, smile and look happy when called upon. Jackie wasn't spared that fate.

Ashton Hawkins

MR. HAWKINS IS EXECUTIVE VICE PRESIDENT AND COUNSEL TO THE TRUSTEES
OF THE METROPOLITAN MUSEUM OF ART

CALIFORNIA, SPRING 1960

She published my most recent book, "Poet and Dancer." She made the book her own—she lived with it; she would do anything for it. She made the most beautiful cover from one of my husband's drawings.

She seemed to know exactly the right thing to do and to say. And yet you did get this feeling of shyness with her—all the social graces you could ever have, but with this shyness. I have the same thing, and I think we understood each other very well. In one of the last notes I had from her, she wrote, "Isn't it wonderful the way our friendship is growing and growing?"

I just finished my most recent manuscript, and she knew that I was going on a trip, and she called me to say, "Can I have it before you go?" I'd like to think that she had it with her, that a part of me could have been there, along with all the people keeping vigil for her on the street.

Ruth Prawer Jhabvala

MS. JHABVALA IS A NEW YORK-BASED AUTHOR

In the early part of the campaign, on a Sunday morning after mass, the Kennedys quietly slipped into the local diner for breakfast. They sat undisturbed. Nobody recognized them. Six months later neither Jackie nor her husband would be able to enjoy that kind of privacy ever again.

A SMALL TOWN IN OREGON. LATE FALL 1959

I first met Jacqueline Kennedy Onassis in a formal way when she became the major figure in organizing support for New York City's beleaguered landmark law and protecting particular buildings, such as Grand Central Terminal, from demolition. One of the photos that I treasure from my years as a public official is of Mrs. Kennedy Onassis, Philip Johnson, Bess Myerson and me taken after we attended a meeting called to save Grand Central. We are walking four abreast down the avenue, all of us knowing that Jackie was the leader and the heart and soul of the movement.

After I left Gracie Mansion in 1989, the Mayor's official residence, and moved to my home in Greenwich Village, I had the privilege and pleasure of hosting a small dinner party for a dozen people including Mrs. Kennedy Onassis and her escort, Maurice Templesman. During dinner, I asked each guest to take a few minutes to introduce themselves. When it was Mrs. Kennedy Onassis' turn, she said quite simply in her distinctive voice, "My name is Jacqueline Kennedy Onassis. I am an editor, and I am now working on a book," which she proceeded to tell us about. She was direct, charmingly modest, and everyone was entranced by her, certainly in part because of her personality and intelligence.

When she was leaving at the end of the evening, she said to me, "I have never had so much fun at a dinner." While I am sure she always left her host with a gracious remark, I do hope she enjoyed the evening, because I know I certainly did.

What I find so remarkable is that under the most difficult of circumstances and with all of the tragedies to which she and her family were subjected, she raised two extraordinary children. John and Caroline are gifted individuals with their mother's modest demeanor and gentility. Because they are the children of President John F. Kennedy and Jacqueline Kennedy Onassis, they are mindful of their place in the hearts of their fellow countrymen. As they say in America, the apple doesn't fall far from the tree.

Edward I. Koch

MR. KOCH IS A FORMER MAYOR OF NEW YORK CITY

Jackie brushes Caroline's hair in the foyer of their Georgetown house.

GEORGETOWN. EARLY FALL 1959

59

J "Jackie? Let's just agree that, if you were married to her, you would have to be the President of the United States." I described her so often in those words, during the years we worked on the six books we did together.

She praised you, if you were her friend, with such warmth and enthusiasm and with such generosity of spirit that you would try anything to please her, anything to merit her esteem.

She expressed herself beautifully, and she liked to write notes to thank you for a lunch or for a small token of friendship sent at Christmas or Valentine's Day or on her birthday, or just sent because it felt good to send her some little thing you knew she'd like.

They were great notes: "I am just bedazzled by your magnificent scarf. I will wear it as an evening dress, as a shawl, I may get a beautiful flagpole and fly it from my apartment as a banner."

"How spiffy is my BEAUTIFUL tie! And what fun I will have wearing it—with maybe one of John's suits which I will appropriate."

"I loved lunch with you SO much. And having the time to talk and walk up Fifth Avenue in the sun. I don't seem to make time enough for that."

"I dream about your book as I subsist on Lean Cuisine and candy bars in beautiful Virginia. I get hungry just thinking about it. My horses live in greatest luxury but my cabin is not famous for gourmet delights."

There were so many things in those notes and letters and postcards that I long to be able to say back to her:
"I think it is *you* who have given me all these sprees of joy…"
"Look how great you are…"
"Look… and praise yourself to the skies."
"You have made me so happy"
"Seeing you was always like champagne."
"Thank you.…"

John Loring

MR. LORING IS DESIGN DIRECTOR AT TIFFANY & CO.

The candidate's wife is being assessed by the local aristocracy at a Democratic rally.

J ehovah would permit no graven images of Himself, and savages feel a part of their soul is stolen when a photograph is taken. What do they do when subjected to flashbulbs? The last time I saw Jacqueline Kennedy Onassis was at a benefit and the cameras were going wild. At one point it was my turn to stand next to the lady, and while I have seen a few such lights, I can testify that my eyes never knew this kind of bombardment before. There is celebrity, and then there is the white heat of celebrity when paparazzi are out, but for sheer impact, for the literal blast of the media at its highest voltage, get your picture taken next to Jackie. It is equal to the blaze of five machine guns turned on you at once.

I remember she stood it with the sad, soldierly dignity of a much-wounded veteran. In the middle of the racket, for the electronic voice of flashes and strobes seems to mount exponentially, I whispered to her—as who does not, since part of the penalty of being Jackie Kennedy Onassis is that everybody wants to offer some bright exchange in her presence?—"Yes," I said to her, "the reason we're all such idiots is these damn lights."

There are a few people in the world whom the media have projected right out of themselves. They will never again find their identity any more than a space probe sent out to explore beyond the solar system will come back to earth. Of this number, Jackie Kennedy may be the first, since history cast her as the leading lady in what must have been the greatest American drama of them all (at least, if drama has the power to make us all react as one). While we are, on balance, a nation more fortunate than most, and not all that many of us have known tragedy in our personal lives, we are close to tragedy through her. In our history she is the only living symbol of Greek drama. Did the shades of Aeschylus and Sophocles agree for once and say, "Let her now be remarried to a Greek who will be a little like one of our mighty blood stained kings"?

If so, they did it for the Greeks, not for us. In our national depths (if we still have any) a part of us will never forgive Jackie Kennedy for marrying Onassis. She had no right to do that, Americans will always feel. She was

CALIFORNIA, SPRING 1960

ours. She did not belong to herself. She was twice ours, once as the most beautiful and romantic legend we ever had in a First Lady; afterward she was ours as the first monumental American widow. We are a country of weeds and frontiers and innovations and hideous designs for mass living, gargantuan corporate structures with all the architectural eclat of a cardboard carton and cancer gulch through all the hours of a universe of day and night TV. We are an overloaded garbage can the size of the universe; we teem, we swarm, we lose ourselves in details and gobble our media like a freak that takes pills. But in retrospect we can say that once we had a romantic heroine and she was married to one of the more handsome men in America, and they were President and First Lady, and so our dream life thrived. We dwelt in an iridescent landscape of secret hopes and daring desires; there was a lift of promise in one's work and the prospect of pleasures after chores. I exaggerate, but then, our dream life lives in the special logic of exaggeration, and so there was something more exciting about America when we had such a heroine, such a beautiful and mysterious lady in such a place. The schizophrenic halves of our nation were bound together. The Hollywood dream life and the superhighways of technology came closer for a little while.

Then the assassinations fell upon us, and the strangest of our American heroines became a Greek heroine. Our nation knew tragedy in the circle of each family as we had not known it since the death of Abraham Lincoln. And we mourned as one nation. We mourned for her as our tragic widow.

Yes, she lost her identity forever. The shy, still strange, doubtless witty, probably decent, much-harried lady of that second self who would only like to do with her life what each of us would like to do with ours—that is, get a little better, a little wiser, a little classier, a little sweeter, and a little more entitled to love—is lost in isolation. Through no fault of hers, she can never rejoin our high-tech humanly reductive race. She may be lonely within, or mature and become splendid, but we will never know, and she will never reach us. All that is left is to photograph the dignity of her shell. We have dispatched her to the gods, and from those divine fields no legend ever returns.

Norman Mailer

MR. MAILER IS A NEW YORK-BASED AUTHOR

The Kennedys recite the Pledge of Allegiance prior to addressing the audience at a California High School.

CALIFORNIA, SPRING 1960

I don't know if you know about the airplane called the *Caroline*. Well, this was an airplane that Jack Kennedy bought for his campaigning. He calculated that it would be cheaper than flying commercial airlines. After he died, the family kept it for a while. I remember that I flew up from Washington to New York in the *Caroline*, and Jackie would be waiting for me and she would hand me the car keys, because Jackie was one of those women who believed that the man should always drive the car. I hardly think anybody is like that anymore.

I know that future historians listening to the tapes of my interviews with her will be puzzled by the clunking sounds. The reason was, in order to get through those evenings, Jackie would have a vast bowl of daiquiris mixed with ice and lemon, and we would drink daiquiris.

I once asked Jack to describe his wife in a single word, and he did—*fey*. I thought it was perfect.

William Manchester

MR. MANCHESTER IS AN AUTHOR AND KENNEDY HISTORIAN

Senator and Mrs. Kennedy. A political team in action. This was before Jackie's pregnancy prevented her from further campaigning.

WASHINGTON STATE. SPRING 1960

Jacqueline Kennedy Onassis was the ultimate American woman of style. She had been preceded by earlier great American women of style who had created through democracy's ennoblement of style a device of class conquest. Fashionable American women had long gained access to titles, aristocratic carriage, and the cultivated manners of the world as a victory of style. American women had also been promoted by media to a status of modern celebrity in their embodiment of grace and glamour, often inflected by Hollywood.

But Mrs. Kennedy achieved characteristics of status that no other American woman had ever attained nor would. In part, her privilege was in becoming First Lady, but she was the First Lady of a mid-century America affluent and hegemonic with the prodigious energy of American post-War industry and culture. She defined and enhanced the image of First Lady and she created the final testament to American style at its eminence. She rejected the blandishments of majesty, preferring instead to engender her style in simplicity and principles of elegance. Mrs. Kennedy was a model of subdued style at the very moment of America's most inflated world power and economy.

While Mrs. Kennedy's style evolved, its apogee was in 1958 through 1963. In fact, Mrs. Kennedy's 1953 wedding dress, designed by the great African-American custom dressmaker Anne Lowe, was a florid creation compared to Mrs. Kennedy's gradual distillation of style in the late 1950s. In close association with her good friend and mentor Diana Vreeland, Mrs. Kennedy reasoned dress as a personal statement and as a fitting expression for a woman on whom national and international attention was a responsibility. Mrs. Kennedy always maintained her allegiance to sportswear and to the modern clothing ideal of American sportswear. Thus, riding clothes, pants, jodhpurs, gingham blouses for Hyannis, and the rudiments of a comfortable basic wardrobe were always evident. Moreover, she translated this ideal into her wardrobe for day and evening, reconciling the elegant simplicity of Givenchy and the reduced silhouettes of the 1960s with the principles she well understood from sportswear. Like Vreeland, Mrs. Kennedy understood the ethos of the working woman, long before the phrase had been known in the 1970s and hackneyed in the 1980s and 1990s.

While the Senator addresses a nearly empty Union Hall of Longshoremen, who seem unimpressed, Jackie chats with one of the members. She too is all but ignored.

COOS BAY, OREGON. FALL 1959

Her evening clothes were brilliant, but simple, seeking out the designers of essence, the disciplined couturiers who complemented austerity with luxury: Cristobal Balenciaga, Madame Grès, Gabrielle Chanel, and Hubert de Givenchy. A later interest in Valentino would not betray these interests, but Mrs. Kennedy's deep devotion to the designers of regimen and realism prevailed during the late 1950s and early 1960s. To some critics, shopping in Paris was a vice, but Mrs. Kennedy's discernment among the many rich options of Paris couture was always about a plainness, a modesty in principle that inexorably defines the couture's best. Similarly, her patronage of Oleg Cassini for clothing and Halston for her legendary pillbox hat was about finding the easy, versatile shapes at the essence of style.

Mrs. Kennedy was an obdurate moralist in the salons of style. A young First Lady captured the American sensibility of style perhaps more than any of the other "women of style" who so readily become the extravagants of personal indulgence and self-spectacle. Refusal—avoiding the superfluous and ostentatious—is the essential trait of her style. Is Mrs. Kennedy our abiding paradigm of style because she was the most exceptionally elegant woman or because she reversed style in America from aspirations to glamour and conspicuousness to a sense of grace closer to the world of Henry David Thoreau than to the European courts? For many enthusiasts and idolaters, Mrs. Kennedy can only have been seen in the mold of conventional women of style. On the contrary, though she captured the heart of Paris and scrupulously bought from the great houses of Paris, Mrs. Kennedy made style American in her reserve and refusal. She was parsimonious with luxury, knowing that its sensuality and charisma were best enjoyed in complement to the relaxed and comfortable. She made high style genuinely American, unlike the ambitious, yearning women before her, in her innate inhibition and casual pragmatism. Hers was consummate American style because it expressed, even at the height of the American hegemony, a spirit honest, unfeigned and discreet.

The Senator and Mrs. Kennedy leave an Elks meeting in California.

Richard Martin

MR. MARTIN IS THE CURATOR OF THE DESIGN INSTITUTE AT
THE METROPOLITAN MUSEUM OF ART

CALIFORNIA. SPRING 1960

71

I prayed and I mourned and I watched, and these were the thoughts that drifted in and out of my mind in a sad stream of consciousness as I sat in St. Ignatius Loyola Church at a funeral I never thought I would be attending—ever. Jackie Kennedy Onassis was not supposed to die. She was not meant to leave us behind to grieve, we who loved and admired and respected her. She was supposed to live forever, luminous and immortal, eternally smiling that angel smile, somehow making us all feel better about ourselves, whether we knew her or not. She was an inspiration to every woman, this extraordinary lady who had endured enough agony and ecstasy to last a dozen lifetimes, who had scaled the peaks joyously and shown us all how to suffer in grace the deep valleys that are the fate of us all.

The priest, every word clear as a bell, called her Jacque-leen, giving her name the French pronunciation she is said to have preferred in the days when she first met John Fitzgerald Kennedy and they fell in love. Jacque-leen didn't last long. It was soon Jackie to the world. A world in her thrall.

Those were the days when Senator and Mrs. John Fitzgerald Kennedy lived a block away from me in Georgetown, and Ethel and Bobby Kennedy and their fast-growing brood lived right across the street. Remembering this, I turned to watch Ethel as she walked up the aisle, bent, pale-faced and heavy-hearted, surrounded by her sons and daughters. How many times had she taken these devastating steps before? Too many.

On the podium, Jackie's beautiful children, Caroline and John, who planned the glorious service, spoke lovingly of their mother; Jackie's friend, Jane Hitchcock, recited the 23rd Psalm; Mike Nichols told of Jackie's spirit of adventure. Maurice Tempelsman, the financier who was her loving companion for the last decade or more, his voice trembling, read the poem, "Ithika," and made his poignant farewells. And in his eulogy, Senator Edward Kennedy, Jackie's brother-in-law, made the most eloquent speech of his life. He caught the essence of Jackie perfectly and almost made her come alive again for the rapt crowd in the church.

I wondered—how many men in her life loved her the way a man in love really loves a woman? Perhaps Jack Kennedy at first, intrigued by the

The time between the end of the Democratic Convention and the start of the general election campaign on Labor Day was the last true carefree and private time the Kennedys were to have until the president's fearful and premature death. They enjoyed themselves enormously, the Senator sailing and playing golf, Jackie arranging picnics and spending time with all the children at the Kennedy compound.

HYANNIS PORT, MASSACHUSETTS. AUGUST 1960

combination of class and beauty, her bearing and sense of style, her effortless ability to beguile and charm. But whatever it was he felt, it didn't last long, and her humiliation began. She took it with her head held high. God alone knows what was going on inside.

To Aristotle Onassis, the Greek tycoon, the beautiful young widow who married him in a move to leave the past behind and move on to a secure present, she was a trophy, the biggest prize of all. I remembered that Jackie helped make Skorpios, neglected until her arrival, an Eden, and that Ari, a fun-loving, life-loving bear of a man whom I liked despite his being self-centered and spoiled, strangely resented her for it. Love had flown, and nothing she could do was right.

So, finally, enter Maurice Tempelsman, the erudite, charming, worldly man who had the brains and the taste and the insight to appreciate the wondrous creature Jackie was. He gave her the love, the support, the refuge and the strength that other men had denied her. "She was so wonderfully lucky to have had you for those years," one of Jackie's friends said to Maurice at Jackie's wake. "No," he said, "I was so wonderfully lucky to have had her."

And weren't we all? I was lucky to be her friend, to have her encourage me and flatter me and never stop asking me through the years to write a book. She would call me and write me little notes (I've saved them all) and sit in my apartment and talk. "You know these people like no one else," she would say. "Write about them, their lives, their ambitions, their lies. Write how nothing *really* is the way it seems. How these women who seem to have it all, are really desperate and trapped." Then she would smile and say, "But if one has to be trapped and unhappy, maybe it's better in sables after all."

At the alter, Jessye Norman sang "Ave Maria"—Jackie's confirmation name was Mary—and outside the sun was shining on the sort of beautiful late-spring day Jackie might have ordered for herself. I was glad. I was sad. I didn't know what I was. I only knew that I thought she was wonderful—and I always will.

Aileen Mehle

MS. MEHLE IS A REGULAR CONTRIBUTOR TO *W* MAGAZINE

Jackie and Caroline continue the games on the porch of the Kennedy summer home after the senator has left for his golf game. "I Can Fly" was Caroline's favorite book then.

HYANNIS PORT, MASSACHUSETTS. AUGUST 1960

75

She was a last link to a certain kind of past, and that is part, but only part, of why we mourn so, Jackie Kennedy *symbolized*—she was a connection to a time, to an old America in which standards were higher and clearer and elegance meant something, a time when elegance was a kind of statement, a way of dressing up the world, and so a generous act. She had manners, the kind that remind us that manners spring from a certain moral view—that you do tribute to the world and the people in it by being kind and showing respect, by sending the note and the flowers, by being loyal, and cheering a friend. She was a living reminder in the age of Oprah that personal dignity is always, still, an option, a choice that is open to you. She was, really, the last aristocrat. Few people get to symbolize a world, but she did, and that world is receding, and we know it and mourn that too.

Those who knew her or watched her from afar groped for the words that could explain their feeling of loss. A friend of hers said, with a soft, sad voice, that what we're losing is what we long for: the old idea of being cultivated. "She had this complex, colorful mind, she loved a turn of phrase. She didn't grow up in front of the TV set, but reading the classics and thinking about them and having thoughts about history. "Oh," he said, "we're losing her kind."

I echoed the sentiment to another of her friends, who cut me off. "She wasn't a kind, she was sui generis." And so she was.

America continues in its generational shift; the great ones of the '50's and '60's, big people of a big era, are going, and too often these days we're saying goodbye. But Jackie Kennedy's death is different. No ambivalence clouds her departure, and that leaves us feeling lonely. America is a lonelier place.

She was too young, deserved more time, and the fact that she didn't get it seems like a new level of unfairness. She never saw her husband grow old, and now she won't see her grandchildren grow up. But just writing these words makes me want to break out of sadness and reach back in time and speak '60's-speak, or at least how the '60's spoke before they turned dark. So I guess I mean I want to speak Kennedyese. I want to say, *Aw listen, kid, don't be glum. What a life she had.*

A great part of the carefree days between the convention and the start of the general election campaign were spent in the water.

HYANNIS PORT, MASSACHUSETTS. AUGUST 1960

77

She herself said something like this to a friend, in a conversation just months ago, when she first knew she was sick. She told him she was optimistic and hoped to live 20 more years. "But even if I have only five years, so what, I've had a great run."

That weekend in November '63, the weekend of the muffled drums, was the worst time for America in the last half of this century. We forget now the shame we felt as a nation at what had happened in Dallas. A President had been murdered, quite savagely, quite brutally, and the whole appalled world was looking and judging. And she redeemed it. She took away the shame by how she acted. She was young, only 34, and only a few days before she'd been covered in her husband's blood—but she came home to Washington and walked down those broad avenues dressed in black, her pale face cleansed and washed clean by trauma. She walked head up, back straight and proud, in a flowing black veil. There was the moment in the Capitol Rotunda, when she knelt with her daughter Caroline. It was the last moment of public farewell, and to say it she bent and kissed the flag that draped the coffin that contained her husband—and a whole nation, a whole world, was made silent at the sight of patriotism made tender. Her Irish husband had admired class. That weekend she showed it in abundance. What a parting gift.

A nation watched, and would never forget. The world watched, and found its final judgement summed up by a young woman, a British journalist who had come to witness the funeral, and filed home: "Jacqueline Kennedy has today given her country the one thing it has always lacked, and that is majesty."

In a remarkable interview she gave Theodore White the following December, she revealed what a tough little romantic she was. "Once, the more I read of history, the more bitter I got. For a while I thought history was something that bitter old men wrote. But then I realized history made Jack what he was. You must think of him as this little boy, sick so much of the time, reading in bed, reading history, reading the Knights of the Round Table, reading Marlborough. For Jack, history was full of heroes— maybe other little boys will see. Men are such a combination of good and bad. Jack had this heroic idea of history, this idealistic view." And she spoke of Camelot and gave the world an image of her husband that is still, for all the revelations of the past three decades, alive. She provided an image of

Here, on a Sunday after church, the Kennedys romp in Nantucket Bay in front of their house in a plastic boat hardly larger than a bathtub. Their enjoyment is obvious.

HYANNIS PORT, MASSACHUSETTS. AUGUST 1960

herself too, perhaps more than she knew. The day before she died, a young schoolteacher in New York City who hadn't even been born when she spoke to Teddy White, told me of his shock that she was leaving us. "I thought she would be like Guinevere," he said, "I thought she would ride off on a horse, in her beautiful silence, and never die."

Her friends saw a great poignance in her, and a great yearning. Behind her shyness there was an enormous receptivity to the sweetness of life and its grace. A few years ago, friends, a couple, gave a small dinner party for two friends who had just married, and Mrs. Onassis was among the guests. It was an elegant New York gathering, a handful of the renowned of show business and media and society, all gathered to dine on the top floor of a skyscraper. The evening was full of laughter and warm toasts, and the next day her hosts received from Mrs. Onassis a handwritten, hand-delivered letter. "How could there be an evening more magical than last night? Everyone is enhanced and touched by being with two people just discovering how much they love each other. I have known and adored (him) for so long, always wishing he would find happiness… Seeing him with (her) and getting to know her, I see he has at last—and she so exceptional, whom you describe so movingly, has too. I am so full of joy for both—I just kept thinking about it all day today. What wonderful soothing hosts you are—what a dazzling gathering of their friends—in that beautiful tower, with New York glittering below…"

I wish we could have taken her, in the city she loved or the capital she graced, and put a flag on her coffin and the coffin on a catafalque, and march it down a great avenue, with an honor guard and a horse that kicks, as Black Jack did, and muffled drums. I wish we could have gone and honored her, those of us who were children when she was in the White House, and our parents who wept that weekend long ago, and our children who have only a child's sense of who and what she was. I wish we could have stood on the sidewalk as the caisson passed, and taken off our hats and explained to our sons and daughters and say, "That is a patriot passing by." I wish I could see someone's little boy, in a knee-length coat, lift his arm and salute.

Peggy Noonan

MS. NOONAN WAS A SPEECHWRITER FOR THE REAGAN AND BUSH ADMINISTRATIONS

A giggling Jackie in a rare moment of total relaxation looks absolutely astonishing in a bathing cap and suit, swim-wear that is now back in style.

HYANNIS PORT, MASSACHUSETTS. AUGUST 1960

I suspect it's the last thing most people would think of, but I've always identified Jackie with pirates. When I first knew her, she seemed fixed on them. She once told me that as a child she had a pirate flag hanging on the wall of her room at Hammersmith Farm in Newport. Her father looked like a pirate. She married a pirate, Ari Onassis.

But what comes to mind most vividly is a pirate party she gave at Hammersmith Farm one autumn afternoon in 1965 for her two children and their Newport friends—a collection of youthful Pells, Grosvenors, Drexels, Warrens and Gardners, some young enough to be attending their first party. Jackie asked me to help organize it, though in fact she had already planned it very carefully in her own mind. The feature was a paper chase that would lead the children down sloping lawns to a treasure chest buried a few yards from the waters of Narragansett Bay. And her inspired notion was this: as soon as the children, having followed various clues, had reached the spot and begun digging for the chest, a boatload of adults dressed up as pirates would appear around the bend and come bustling ashore to reclaim their treasure. She had a list of pirates—six of us, as I recall, including Senator Claiborne Pell. There would be a fight, and the children would drive us back into the sea. "That's the scenario?" she said, phrasing her sentence in the form of a questions, as she often did. She then said, "I have a longboat for you."

We went shopping together for the contents of the treasure chest. She nearly cleared out one gift shop we visited: strings of fake pearls; brass ashtrays; key chains. She got a treasure chest—a quite substantial one, with brass studs and a leather strap. I don't recall the exact circumstance of burying it, but I do remember that she put a rubber snake on top. She said, "As soon as the children see it, it will be time for you pirates to come around the rocks in your longboat. I'll signal you from the shore."

Her enthusiasm, her childlike delight in all this, was irresistible. She wanted me to write a little story that she could read to the children the next day —a story of how the treasure came to be buried, and with hints of where

Jackie was an enthusiastic amateur painter. She painted in a primitive Grandma Moses style and some of her paintings are enchanting. Her gift to JFK returning from the Democratic Convention was a painting depicting him as "Washington Crossing the Delaware," but wearing a Napoleonic tunic. Here she is with Caroline in a guest room of the Kennedy house.

HYANNIS PORT, MASSACHUSETTS. SEPTEMBER 1960

83

the treasure might be found. Would I do this? Of course. I stayed up most of the night working on a kind of "diary" kept by one of the pirates.

On the day of the party, Jackie came with her paintbox and various items of clothing to sharpen us up as pirates. Once in the longboat, we stood on our oars as we waited for the signal from Jackie. I could see her, encircled by children, on the lawn up by the house. Then the children broke the cluster around her and, following the paper clues, eventually streamed toward the shoreline. At some point, shovels were produced. Soon enough the treasure chest was unearthed. Jackie waved us on.

The timing was perfect. I have often thought about how terrifying the sight of us must have been to the children—we were waving our swords and shouting "Yo-ho-ho!" Some of the children turned and scampered off toward their mothers. Others sat and sobbed. Some were not so startled, though. I stepped off the bow of the longboat onto a shoreline boulder. There I was addressed by Caroline Kennedy, who was then about eight. "Well, I know who you are," she said, and stamped her foot.

The older children attacked us with shrill cries. We pirates succumbed gracefully and, I think, quite quickly. What sobbing there was subsided. But for Jackie the spirit of the afternoon was not quite done. She persuaded her Secret Service agent to walk the plank off Hammersmith Farm Dock. He went in with a tremendous splash.

At the end, close to sunset, I remember her in a circle of children. They had asked her to read the diary to them again—as if to retain a bit more of that enchanted afternoon. The bell of her hair obscured her features as she bent over that absurd text. I could barely hear her voice as she whispered to them how something was going to come for them from the sea.

George Plimpton

MR. PLIMPTON IS WRITER AND EDITOR OF *THE PARIS REVIEW*

The Kennedys on Election Day, November 8, 1960.

HYANNIS PORT, MASSACHUSETTS. NOVEMBER 8, 1960

I am honored to serve as Honorary Chair for the exhibit, *A Tribute to Jackie*, which will benefit the Leukemia Society's Jacqueline Kennedy Onassis Lymphoma Research Fund. Leukemia is a terrible disease which claims the lives of thousands each year.

Jackie was very kind to me on numerous occasions. She wrote me a most touching letter when my husband was shot, a time I really needed it. She also wrote when we came home from the hospital—and at other times she knew were difficult. I will always be grateful to her.

I believe Jackie would be pleased to know that her private battle with lymphoma has brought public attention to finding a cure for this disease. I am honored to be a part of this special effort, and I hope and pray a cure will be found.

Nancy Reagan

MRS. REAGAN IS A FORMER FIRST LADY OF THE UNITED STATES AND
HONORARY CHAIR OF "A TRIBUTE TO JACKIE"

John F. Kennedy was elected President of the United States shortly after 12:30 pm on Wednesday, November 9, 1960, the day after Election Day, by a narrow 100,000 votes. The world's press was now waiting for the president-elect at the Hyannis Port armory. I realized this would be the only chance I would ever get to photograph the entire Kennedy clan. They would never be together again in one small place like this.

HYANNIS PORT, MASSACHUSETTS, NOVEMBER 1960

W We all have memories of the elegant hostess in the White House, the loving mother and the brave widow who rallied the country after that terrible November day. But when I look back, I remember a woman who was not at all pretentious but seemed very down to earth to me.

One of my favorite personal memories of Mrs. Kennedy was almost two lifetimes ago in the 1950's. It was during one of the joint sessions of Congress. Her husband was a senator from Massachusetts and my father was a senator from Texas. My father always wanted me to be able to hear important speeches but frequently his best tickets went to constituents. Senator Kennedy may have had the same philosophy. So there we were in the gallery, with our knees up to our chins, sharing an aisle step for a seat. We both could not help but laugh at our situation. A few years later when she was the sophisticated First Lady, I would remember her warmth and kindness to a shy, gawky teenager.

As you can see, I share the admiration the country has for this elegant woman, but I will always remember her generous warmth and unassuming nature in those days long ago.

Lynda Johnson Robb

MRS. ROBB IS THE DAUGHTER OF PRESIDENT AND LADY BIRD JOHNSON AND
THE WIFE OF VIRGINIA SENATOR CHUCK ROBB

President-elect and Mrs. Kennedy, on their way to the Inauguration, leave their Georgetown house for the last time. That day they will move into the White House.

GEORGETOWN, JANUARY 20, 1961

There was an unwritten law among all of us at Doubleday—that we would never publicly discuss Jackie. The genesis of this posture was nothing more than a desire to shield her, but the flip side of this protective gesture was the fact that few people understood how committed and talented she was at the work she chose to do.

Think for a moment of the irony of the fact that she was clearly *the* first lady, unto herself and original in everything she did from her manner of thinking, speaking, and writing, to her extraordinary dignity and courage in the face of horrendous tragedy. Why then, given these sterling qualities, would she not be just as formidable as a laborer in the literary vineyards? Of course she was, though there were some who couldn't quite believe it. Many were surprised to hear that she actually came to the office, attended meetings, and worked hard. More to the point, and equally mystifying is the fact that some could not fathom that Jackie's style and taste quite naturally translated into an instinct for acquiring and publishing books that were not only sui generis, but financially remunerative.

Am I trying to tell you that along with her unending reservoir of talent Jackie was also a businesswoman? No. But I can say that she reveled in her books becoming money makers. The difference was that making money wasn't what fueled her passion; publishing good, interesting books motivated her. And such was her uncanny instinct that many of her projects became truly popular while also retaining the formidable quality for which she was famed.

Stephen Rubin

MR. RUBIN IS PRESIDENT AND PUBLISHER OF DOUBLEDAY BOOKS

Following JFK's by now historic inaugural speech, the crowd, including President Eisenhower, Vice Presidents Nixon and Johnson, the entire Senate and House, the Supreme Court and other dignitaries, leave the inaugural platform. Somehow Jackie, wearing a white pill box hat and white coat stands out from the large crowd mostly dressed in black.

THE CAPITOL. JANUARY 20, 1961

She was a woman of fierce independence. Of course she was famously beautiful and elegant, and she fascinated and enchanted her age. But one recalls above all the quiet but implacable determination, amid the uncontrollable blazes of publicity, to live her own life.

Her father, Black Jack Bouvier, was a swashbuckler. Her mother was a very proper society matron. She was brought up at a time—the 1940s, and in a place—Newport—where young ladies were taught to conceal their intelligence lest it frighten young men away. She observed the conventions, but underneath a shy exterior developed cool judgement of people and an ironical slant on life.

In the early 1950s, she met another ironist, John Fitzgerald Kennedy. Their marriage was a notable moment in the social history of the United States: at last the Irish were accepted in Newport.

Jacqueline Kennedy took to her new political life more easily than her Newport friends expected. Like her husband, she was an idealist, and like him, an idealist without illusions. She came to like politicians and their free and easy talk, and she came rather to like campaigning. Bursting upon the electorate in 1960, the handsome couple seemed the embodiment of youth, and rather daring in a nation ruled by tired old men.

She added more than decoration. Jack Kennedy always sought her assessments of people, and sometimes asked her to carry out confidential missions. When, for example, he wanted to talk to John Kenneth Galbraith and me, but did not want to disquiet his possessive and overworked campaign staff, Jacqueline would make the call and set up the meeting.

Once her husband had been elected President, she wondered how she could best play her role as presidential wife (she detested the term First Lady, regarding it as undemocratic). Her expertise lay in the arts, and her aim was to use the White House to honor artistic achievement. Soon Casals, Stravinsky, Robert Frost, Irving Berlin and Leonard Bernstein were presidential guests. Jackie saw the White House itself not as a private residence, but as a posses-

President and First Lady Jacqueline Kennedy wind their way up Pennsylvania Avenue from the Capitol to the White House, where they will watch the Inaugural Parade. The open car is an eerie reminder of the later, tragic events.

THE CAPITOL. JANUARY 20, 1961

sion of the American people, and she very efficiently organized a redecoration and refurnishing designed to renew the historical continuities.

To those of us on the White House staff, the Kennedys appeared an affectionate couple, delighting in each other and their two children. No one can know the inwardness of a marriage, but despite latterday tales of women parading through the White House, theirs seemed increasingly close. The President could be a solicitous husband. I remember him asking me after the loss of their third child, whether I could get Adlai Stevenson to send a note of condolence: "Jackie is very fond of Adlai, and hasn't heard a word from him."

Then came Dallas. In the dark weeks and months afterward, Jacqueline and her brother-in-law, Robert, were drawn together in grief. He became the protective element in her life. Seeking privacy for her children and for herself, she moved to New York and began a new career as an editor in a publishing house, a job for which her critical eye and flawless taste admirably equipped her. She was proud of Robert Kennedy in his opposition to the war in Vietnam, but hated it when he decided to run for President. "They will do to him what they did to Jack," she said to me in March 1968. In June, "they" did as she predicted. Three months later, seeking a new protection, she married Aristotle Onassis.

After Onassis died, Jacqueline returned to her quiet, highly disciplined life: winter in New York; riding in New Jersey or Virginia in spring and autumn; summer in Martha's Vineyard. An excellent mother, she raised unspoiled children and taught them how to elude the paparazzi. Both are lawyers; Caroline has co-authored a book on the Bill of Rights and now has three children of her own.

In her middle years, Jacqueline was more fascinating than ever. Her finely modelled face resisted age. She always had the seductive habit of giving undivided attention to the person with whom she was talking. Her humor gleamed, and her zest for life never flagged. She was a great reader and loved the theater.

She followed politics and remained an ardent, liberal Democrat to the end. In 1992 she acquired a new friend in Hillary Rodham Clinton. They

Jackie, wearing a glittering gown and a dazzling smile, waits to enter the presidential box at the Inaugural Ball.

THE ARMORY, WASHINGTON, D.C. JANUARY 20, 1961

lunched together a couple of times during the campaign, hit it off at once, and kept in close touch thereafter.

The illness struck unexpectedly last December. Doctors diagnosed it as lymphoma in January. She seemed cheery and hopeful, perhaps to keep up the spirits of her friends. "I feel it is a kind of hubris," she told me. "I have always been proud of keeping so fit. I swim, and I jog, and I do my push-ups and walk around the reservoir, and I gave up smoking forty years ago—and now this suddenly happens." She laughed as she talked. Chemotherapy, she added, was not too bad; she could read a book while it was administered. The doctors said that in 50 percent of cases, lymphoma could be stabilized.

She bore the last ordeal with characteristic gallantry and with never a word of complaint. She died as she lived, in grace and dignity, "a very classy dame," as they say in New York. Henry James would have understood her. She will be remembered as the American woman at her best: brave, disciplined, ironical, imperturbable, filled with a vivid sense of the potentiality and the sadness of life.

Arthur Schlesinger, Jr.

MR. SCHLESINGER WAS A KENNEDY ADMINISTRATION ADVISOR

The First Lady in the presidential box during the Inaugural Ball.

WASHINGTON, D.C. JANUARY 20, 1961

97

Throughout the 41 years I knew her, Jacqueline Kennedy Onassis never failed to surprise me.

With the radiant personality and beauty that dazzled all who met her for the first time or the hundredth time;

With the unfailing good cheer and sly humor with which she entered wholeheartedly into Kennedy family activities, from political campaigns to touch football games;

With the extraordinary strength and courage in the face of ugly tragedy that enabled her, of all people, to comfort others devastated by the loss of her husband, and later her brother-in-law;

With the dogged determination that she devoted to the successful rearing and protection of her two wonderful children under difficult circumstances; and

With the genuine enthusiasm and interest that she constantly displayed in her work and that of others, in her friends old and new, and in causes large and small.

I will miss her always. We all will.

Theodore C. Sorenson

MR. SORENSON WAS A SPEECHWRITER FOR JOHN F. KENNEDY DURING
HIS PRESIDENCY

HYANNIS PORT, MASSACHUSETTS. SUMMER 1961

In 1964, while Jacqueline Bouvier Kennedy was still secluded in her year of mourning, I wrote a long article about this woman I barely knew. As a journalistic assignment, it consisted of reporting the views of friends, relatives, adversaries, politicians, and various public figures on a question that much of the world's media seemed to be asking at the time. What would this thirty-five-old widow do with her life?

Most people said she should play an international, public role. Serving as an ambassador to France, becoming a kind of glamorous Eleanor Roosevelt, or marrying Adlai Stevenson were all on the list.

A few others, especially friends and relatives, thought she had done enough for the world already. A White House correspondent said that, in her role as widow, she had saved the country's sanity by behaving with a sense of history, dignity and courage throughout the complicated events surrounding the death and funeral. Robert Kennedy reacted with a kind of laissez-faire admiration. "Jackie has always kept her own identity," he explained, "and been different."

As for the subject herself—she wasn't saying. While still in the White House, she had reacted with humor to similar questions about her future. "I'll just retire to Boston," she had said, "and try to convince John, Jr. that his father was once the president." Since her year of mourning excluded all interviews, the first clue to her future plans was her interest in the continuation of her husband's work. "He changed our world," she said firmly, "and I hope people will remember him and miss him all their lives." The second was her future. "I was reading Carlyle," she told a reporter, "and he said you should do the duty that lies nearest you. And the thing that lies nearest me is the children."

In retrospect, the most interesting thing about the suggestions for her future was what they left out. With the possible exception of Robert Kennedy, no one even mentioned the idea that she might lead a life of her own. With feminist hindsight, I realize that neither I nor anyone I interviewed was paying her the honor of considering her as a separate human being; as the person she was and would have been, whether or not she had married a future

Jackie with her daughter Caroline and her kittens relaxes on the lawn of Kennedy compound. Although she is the First Lady, she seems to remain simple and uncomplicated.

president. True, she must have been changed by those Kennedy years and all the personal and historical events they contained, but she was still more than the sum of them. Yet we behaved as if she could not (or should not) create any future independent of the powerful Kennedy image.

It was this refusal to see her as a separate woman that increased the public shock when she married Aristotle Onassis. Without an understanding of her own problems and daily life, not to mention the penalties of just existing as the most famous living symbol of the Kennedy era, her second marriage just didn't make sense.

Even when she was alone again after Onassis's death, the speculation about her future plans only seemed to split in two. Would she become a Kennedy again (that is, more political, American and serious) or remain an Onassis (that is, more social, international, and simply rich)?

What no one predicted was her return to the publishing world she had entered briefly after college—to the kind of job she could have had years ago, completely on her own. And that's exactly what she did.

Despite all of us, however, she gradually found her own life.

In 1975, shortly after Onassis's death, Dorothy Schiff, then the successful publisher of the New York *Post*, invited Jackie to lunch to suggest that she consider running for the U.S. Senate against Daniel Patrick Moynihan. Jackie quickly refused that suggestion, but spent the afternoon enthusiastically touring the *Post*'s editorial offices and press room instead. As she explained to Dorothy Schiff, the day brought back good memories of her early career as a young newspaper reporter in Washington. About the same time, she contributed a nicely written but unsigned piece to *The New Yorker* on the opening of the International Center of Photography, a project of her friend Cornell Capa. But neither of these events prepared many of her friends, much less the public, for the decision she soon announced: she would join the Viking Press as a consulting editor. Media commentators seemed both shocked and skeptical. Neither of her husbands had been in publishing. What made her think she could go off on a career of her own? There was much media speculation about her salary and how long she would pursue this new whim. Like parents who couldn't believe their

HYANNIS PORT, MASSACHUSETTS, SUMMER 1961

child was old enough for a first day at school, camera crews and reporters lined up on the sidewalk to record her first day at work.

Despite this public skepticism, she continued to work there four days a week for two years, phoning in conscientiously for messages on her one day off. She went to editorial meetings, suggested ideas and authors, got her own coffee, made her own phone calls, waited at the Xerox machine to do her own copying, worked on a variety of book projects, and made ten thousand dollars a year.

By the time she moved to Doubleday, she had become a full-time associate editor. She could work at home or in the office, or be out doing research and having author's lunches, with less danger of being accused of dilettantism. Her own apartment floor became the space covered by Atget, the French photographer whose collection she edited, or other book layouts. But many people at all levels in publishing were surprised to pick up the phone and hear her unmistakable voice on the line, without benefit of secretarial announcement. And many more in the world at large were surprised when they learned that she was traveling in order to research ideas, seeking out authors, arranging book promotion events or still working at all.

I don't mean to suggest that the Most Famous Woman in the World was just like everyone else. On the contrary, she was like no one else. Part of her uniqueness was an ability to distance herself from her public image, to ignore the obsessive interest of strangers, and to refuse to read most of what is written about her.

Her example poses interesting questions for each of us to ask ourselves: given the options of using Kennedy power or living the international lifestyle of an Onassis, how many of us would have chosen to return to our own talents and less spectacular careers? How many of us would have the strength to choose work over derived influence?

In the long run, her insistence on work that is her own may be more helpful to other women than any use of the conventional power she declined.

Gloria Steinem

MS. STEINEM IS AN AUTHOR AND EDITOR AND PUBLISHER OF *MS.* MAGAZINE

The First Lady descends the stairs of the Elysee Palace, home of the French President, where she had just charmed General de Gaulle, an otherwise dour and imposing figure. Before leaving Paris, Jackie would become the toast of the town.

PARIS. JUNE 1961

105

Once in a lifetime a person of fairness, intelligence, street smarts and exceptional charm enters our lives. Jackie Kennedy Onassis was such a person.

As chairman and fellow board member of Jackie's of the Municipal Art Society, I worked closely with her for many years to make New York a more liveable city. She never tired, never wavered and never gave up her optimism that we could make the city more comfortable and aesthetically beautiful.

I miss her.

Stephen Swid

MR. SWID IS CHAIRMAN OF THE MUNICIPAL ART SOCIETY

The party to honor the Kennedys was Paris' party of the year. The icons of High Society of that sophisticated city were fighting for invitations to the event. Here Jackie, accompanied by Mrs. Charles de Gaulle, is appraised by Parisians. Shades of West Virginia.

PARIS. JUNE 1961

M My last encounter with Jacqueline Kennedy Onassis was in Boston in 1992 on the occasion of receiving the John F. Kennedy Profiles in Courage Award. It was a moment of reminiscing for both of us as we had grown up on Long Island and had many mutual friends, yet had not seen each other since those early days of youth. Obviously for both of us life had changed dramatically in terms of careers in the public eye, but what impressed me most was the great pride and warmth she expressed while speaking of her children. I am sure the public forgets that persons in the limelight are as human as they, and for us our children are more important than all the power and recognition a world bestows upon us. Jacqueline Kennedy Onassis was far more than the ultimate personification of glamour and sophistication in a public figure. She was devoted to family, the arts and the less fortunate—a mix that makes me grateful to have been counted among her friends.

Jackie looked absolutely stunning at that ball. Those who were there still talk about the event.

Lowell Weicker, Jr.

MR. WEICKER IS PRINCIPAL AT DRESSING-LIERMANN-WEICKER AND
THE FORMER GOVERNOR OF CONNECTICUT

PARIS. JUNE 1961

I did not know Mrs. Onassis well, but our paths did occasionally cross—literally. She enjoyed riding in Somerset County, where I was born and raised and learned to ride.

I will never forget the first time I met her. I was a teenager; she, a young widow. We were both riding in the hills of Somerset County, and I remember how beautifully she rode and how elegant she looked in her white britches.

She stopped to talk, which could easily have overwhelmed me. But she was so gracious, I was immediately put at ease.

I have to confess, my horse put her to the test. He had a very unattractive habit of foaming at the mouth—a habit he could not curb even in her presence.

Without warning, he lay his head in her lap and smeared her with green slime from her hips to her knees. But she seemed not to notice; she just smiled and turned her horse around.

My horse, of course, did a repeat performance on her other leg. But she continued to be extremely gracious, saving me from embarrassment and my horse from a good talking to.

Over the years, we would meet again. But my most vivid memory remains my first, when this gracious woman showed both my horse and me the stuff of which true thoroughbreds are made.

Christine Todd Whitman

CHRISTINE TODD WHITMAN IS THE GOVERNOR OF NEW JERSEY

The meeting between the young president and chairman Krushchev had been bitter. Krushchev had tried to bully and threaten JFK who had remained calm. But that night at Castle Schoenbrunn a different Nikita emerged. Totally captivated by Jackie he could hardly contain his enthusiasm, bubbling over with charm and anecdotes.

VIENNA, JUNE 1961

Star Behind the Scenes

Bill Moyers's current leading nonfiction bestseller *Healing and the Mind*, would not have come into existence had it not been for the conviction of his editor that the subject was one of transcendent public interest.

"I told her, 'I don't think these interviews will translate into a book,' " he told *PW* one day last week, calling from Austin, Tex., one of his stops during a tour for the book, which is currently up to 450,000 copies in print. "She said I was wrong. 'The subject will,' she said."

So far, just an enthusiastic author talking about a prescient editor. What makes this case rather different is that the editor in question happens to be Doubleday's secret weapon: not only an editor with a top bestseller (and another last year, Edvard Radzinsky's *The Last Tsar*) but a person with an aura that extends far beyond publishing: Jacqueline Kennedy Onassis.

Getting to interview Onassis is not quite like any other such occasion in this seasoned interviewer's experience. She simply does not give interviews, and only a hint that she might be willing to drop the ban just this once (reportedly at the urging of Doubleday president Stephen Rubin, whose house is having a spectacularly good year thus far) gave us the encouragement to proceed. There were many ground rules: No tape recorder. No camera. She must be allowed to have a sense of the questions to be asked, which must be strictly limited to her professional life, and the prerogative to refuse to answer. She must be given the chance to okay her quotes. And she must be accompanied at the interview by a trusted associate—in this case Marly Rusoff, vice-president and associate publisher, with whom she has developed a close professional relationship.

The interview took place in Rusoff's office, which, unlike Onassis's own, boasts a couple of small sofas. Promptly at the appointed hour she appeared —a slight, stylish figure in a black pinstripe suit worn over a dark gray silk blouse, a heavy antique gold chain with a silver star pendant around her neck; in her arms she carries a stack of books to show us. The gaze from her gray-blue eyes is direct; her hair, in the familiar glossy shape, frames a com-

The Kennedys came to London to officiate at the baptism of the Radziwill's newborn son. The president was to be the godfather. Here, at the party in their honor, the First Lady awaits her guests...and introduces the pill box hat to the U.K.

LONDON, ENGLAND. JUNE 1961

plexion that is ruddy rather than delicate. When she speaks her voice is low and cultivated, but far from the ethereal whisper of her imitators.

Perhaps because she is unaccustomed to this sort of interview, the beginning is a little awkward—monosyllabic replies to questions are common, followed by a dawning realization that more was required: "This isn't just a question-and-answer sort of thing, is it?" she asked.

Assured that it wasn't, she talked more freely. She had come into publishing "for the obvious reasons—I'd majored in literature, I had many friends in publishing, I love books, I've known writers all my life."

One of those friends in publishing was Thomas Guinzburg, then president of Viking Press before it became part of Penguin, who invited Onassis aboard as consulting editor in the fall of 1975. She was there for just two years—and recalls working on only two or three significant books there, including a novel about Sally Hemings, the slave with whom Thomas Jefferson had an affair, written by Barbara Chase-Riboud, a book of Matthew Brady's Lincoln pictures from the original glass plates and a book on Russian style (a continuing passion)—before her past rose up again to haunt her in a dramatic way.

Guinzburg, without consulting her, she says, had bought a novel by British author Jeffrey Archer, called *Shall We Tell The President?*, in which her brother-in-law, Sen. Edward Kennedy, becomes president and is the target of an assassination attempt. She resigned immediately, and it is clear that memories of the incident are still upsetting to her.

In any case, she was not at liberty for long. Another old publishing friend, John Sargent, then Doubleday president, asked her if she would care to join his company, and she did, with the beginning title of associate editor. "I enjoyed publishing, and wanted to go on," she says. Another factor that helped her decide to make Doubleday her publishing home was that Nancy Tuckerman, previously her social secretary at the White House, already worked there—and still does. Onassis came aboard early in 1978, and, as befitted her associate editor status, was awarded a small windowless office.

She has now been at Doubleday for 15 years, and although the image never fades from the public mind, the novelty of her role as a working woman has long worn off. Her title is now senior editor, her office (which we do eventually get to see, cluttered with cartons ready for Doubleday's move from 666 Fifth Avenue to its new building at Broadway and 45th Street) has a window, though it is no more than 12 feet square—and she edits an average of at least a dozen books a year. They are an eclectic mix, predominantly nonfiction, reflecting a thoroughly cosmopolitan mind and an abiding interest in the arts, particularly music, ballet and the visual arts. Some of her titles are surprising, some not, but all have in common a keen attention to their visual appeal, frequently a touch of exoticism. A particular favorite, which she caresses lovingly, is the lavishly illustrated *A Second Paradise: Indian Courtly Life 1590 1947* by Naveen Patnaik, whose *The Garden of Life. An Introduction to the Healing Plants of India* is due out later this year.

"I'm drawn to books that are out of regular experience," says Onassis, asked to sum up her particular interest. "Books of other cultures, ancient histories. I'm interested in the arts in general, especially the creative process. I'm fascinated by hearing artists talk about their craft. To me, a wonderful book is one that takes me on a journey into something I didn't know before."

That curiosity is something that has driven her toward some of the books she is most pleased to have published. It is through Onassis, for instance, that Egyptian Nobel Prize-winning novelist Naguib Mahfouz found publication in this country. "When I read in the paper that this Egyptian had won the Nobel Prize, I thought, 'We've got to have that,' " she says, and right away began planning with Bantam Doubleday Dell's then-CEO Alberto Vitale how it could be managed. She adds: "I've always loved the cultures of the Mediterranean, and I'd lived in Greece" (throwaway remarks like this can cause double takes), "and it clicked with some other Mediterranean writers I very much admired—Kazantzakis, for instance."

But how did she know what Mahfouz's work was like, since it was unavailable in this country? "It was available in French translation, and I read that." Then an indication of how the Onassis network operates. "I finally reached him through David Morse, former head of the International Labor Organization, himself a Nobel winner; I knew he'd know how to contact him, and he did. No, I never got to meet Mahfouz—he doesn't travel—but we corresponded." As a result of her efforts, Doubleday bought out the Cairo Trilogy (*Palace Walk*, *Palace of Desire and Sugar Street*) at the heart of Mahfouz's work, and that in turn led to 15 more of his fictional works appearing as Anchor paperbacks.

She sits beside us on the sofa, thrusting the Cairo Trilogy volumes into our hands. "Aren't they lovely? These were designed by Alex Gottfryd [the late Doubleday art director]. See how each cover has an antique photograph from a different era, reflecting the book's contents?"

An interest in the look and feel of any book she edits is of particular importance to Onassis. She speaks often of two of Doubleday's current art and design directors, Peter Kruzan and Mary Sarah Quinn ("So talented"), and of how much she enjoys working with them on her books. Among her current titles, the Moyers book, for instance, has an image by Georgia O'Keeffe as its cover art—"That's the first time the O'Keeffe estate allowed a picture of hers to be used on any book that wasn't of her own work," she enthuses. And looking at the current novel *Poet and Dancer* by Ruth Prawer Jhabvala, which Onassis also edited, she again exclaims over the cover, a painting by the author's husband of the view from their New York apartment—"It's like an Indian miniature."

Another recent cover on which she is particularly keen is that for *The Last Tsar: The Life and Death of Nicholas II*, which shows Tsar Nicholas sitting sadly on a tree stump in a forest, while Bolshevik guards watch him in the background. "I'm sure it helped sell the book," she says, then shows us a much less evocative cover for the English edition of the book (where it did not sell nearly as well).

"She has a wonderful sense of the aesthetics of a book," says Moyers of his editor. "She cares about the way it looks on a bookstore shelf, on the table at home, in the reader's hands. Every book she does bears her own imprint." And it's certainly true that the dozen or so Onassis books we saw were exceptionally handsome, often in off-beat shapes, or with individual decorations in page numbers and chapter headings. "I want my books to look as beautiful as possible," she says, adding, "Perhaps it's a reaction against the time when Doubleday books used to be quite bad." (A reference to Nelson Doubleday's time, when the company's books were notorious for their low quality.)

Onassis's interests reach in sometimes surprising directions. She takes us through *The Cartoon History of the Universe*, a comic-book paperback by Larry Gonick she published in 1990. (She found the artist through a friend.) It is in vivid comic-strip style but, she insists, "It's very accurate, and a much better account of how civilization developed than many more serious ones I've read." She has worked with *Rolling Stone* publisher Jann Wenner on putting together an anthology of the best pieces to appear in the magazine during the past 25 years, each with an introduction by the writer on how the article came to be written. Like Moyers, Wenner didn't see at first a book in the idea, "but I convinced him," she says. It will appear in September.

Her interest in *Rolling Stone* was aroused by one of its writers, Jonathan Cott ("I love the way his mind works, and we do a lot of books together"). Two already published are The Search for Om Sety, the story of a mysterious Englishwoman who dreamed of a classical temple and then actually discovered it, and *Isis and Osiris*.

Another friendship, with singer Carly Simon, a summertime neighbor on Martha's Vineyard, led to a series of children's books. "We originally thought of a memoir, but she wanted to do children's books, and she came upon one she'd written for her children, called *Amy the Dancing Bear*." That was followed by two more, and a new one, *The Nighttime Chauffeur*, about New York's Central Park, will be out this fall. Ballet star Gelsey Kirkland, whom Onassis introduced with her bestselling *Dancing on My Grave* seven years ago, will be doing a series of young adult books about a girl learning to be a ballerina ("Young girls are always fascinated either by ballet or horses," muses Onassis. "I was fascinated by both.")

Her artistic tastes embrace several kinds of music, and she has done books with both Michael Jackson (the bestselling *Moonwalk*) and classical composer Andrè Previn (*No Minor Chords*, on his early musical life in Hollywood), about whom she says, "He's one of the great raconteurs, comparable to Lenny Bernstein or Martha Graham." Talking of Martha Graham, she has also published that formidable dancer/choreographer's Blood Memory. In the visual arts, she's done *Learning to Look*, a memoir by the celebrated British critic John Pope-Hennessy, and *Stanford White's*

New York by David Lowe ("David really searched the archives on that one, and found some great photos that had never been seen before").

Recent and contemporary history are also among Onassis's interests. "If you live through for a time, it crystallizes later for you, and you want to know more about it," she says. She is talking of the forthcoming *Paris After the Liberation* by Anthony Beevor and Artemis Cooper, and adds: "I don't exactly remember it, but a few years later I was at school there, and it was still very much the same city." *The Cost of Courage* by former Congressman Carl Elliott and *Taming the Storm: The Life and Times of Judge Frank Johnson and the South's Fight over Civil Rights* by Jack Bass were both books she encouraged their authors to write. "These are extraordinary people, and subjects that people should care about," she says. Never mind about their comparatively short life in hardcover: "They'll both be forever in Anchor."

Onassis seeks out most of her books, calling or writing their authors, dealing with agents as necessary. Is it hard for her to deal with agents? Perhaps deliberately misunderstanding the reason for the question, she responds: "I certainly don't think dealing with authors and agents is very hard." She concedes that "I don't work with agents as much as some editors, perhaps —though sometimes when something crosses their desk, I hope they think of me, and say, 'Oh, she might like that.' "

She is in the office three days a week (and when she is, she usually eats at her desk, unless she has a restaurant date with an agent or author). She takes longer-than-usual summer vacations on Martha's Vineyard. There she reads for duty and for pleasure, sometimes those long works everyone promises themselves they'll read. When asked for a sampling of recent pleasure reading, Onassis responds: "Gibbon's *Decline and Fall*. Yes, seriously. Proust? I'd read that long ago." Among more contemporary works, she's just finished, and admired, Abba Eban's *Personal Witness*.

Obviously she could have an enormous impact upon her books if she would publicly push them, but she is wary of that, though "I'll go to a publication party if it will help." And in fact she has appeared, in the past year, at parties for both Radzinsky and Moyers, agreeing to be photographed at the latter with a bevy of visiting booksellers. Rusoff says

Onassis particularly enjoys booksellers, regarding them as key people in the dissemination of ideas within the culture.

Could she imagine having her own imprint at Doubleday? She shakes her head. "One of the things I like about publishing is that you don't promote the editor—you promote the book and the author," she says. On the current state of publishing, "I have no profound thoughts. But I'm always optimistic that people will buy good books. There's nothing to complain about; I love my colleagues here, I love Doubleday." (A feeling that is reciprocated: "I don't know what we'd do without her," says president Stephen Rubin.)

Is it more difficult than it used to be, now that the list at Doubleday has been severely pruned, to get some of her kinds of books through the editorial meetings (where, yes, she does have to speak on their behalf). "No, it's *easier* now," she says firmly. "When any organization becomes more efficient, it helps; it means you don't waste your time. Steve is decisive and quick—you know just where you stand."

Of her qualities as an editor from the writer's point of view, Moyers says: "She has a wonderful sense of humor, and is a lot of fun to work with. She doesn't hover, though she'll call when you're falling behind. More important, she'll drop you a note when things are going really well. It's really a creative collaboration. She works very hard at it." His books, transcribed interviews, haven't called for much line editing, "but she's made key suggestion for changes in my introductory texts." Above all, he says, "she doesn't over-manage you. She has an intuitive sense of the author's role."

That intuition, Moyers feels, extends to seeing possibilities where not even the author does. Onassis had called him after his celebrated TV interviews with Joseph Campbell (whom she knew, of course) to suggest there could be a book in them. "I didn't think so, but she insisted," says Moyers. It became the bestselling *The Power of Myth*. The same thing happened with *The World of Ideas*. "I'll never say no again if she thinks there's a book in anything I do," says Moyers.

John F. Baker

MR. BAKER IS THE EDITORIAL DIRECTIOR OF *PUBLISHERS WEEKLY*

We are joined here today at the site of the eternal flame, lit by Jacqueline Kennedy Onassis 31 years ago, to bid farewell to this remarkable woman whose life will forever glow in the lives of her fellow Americans.

Whether she was soothing a nation grieving for a former President or raising the children with the care and the privacy they deserve, or simply being a good friend, she seemed always to do the right thing in the right way.

She taught us by example about the beauty of art, the meaning of culture, the lessons of history, the power of personal courage, the nobility of public service, and, most of all, the sanctity of family.

God gave her very great gifts and imposed upon her great burdens. She bore them all with dignity and grace and uncommon sense. In the end she cared most about being a good mother to her children, and the lives of Caroline and John leave no doubt that she was that, and more.

Hillary and I are especially grateful that she took so much time to talk about the importance of raising children away from the public eye, and we will always remember the wonderful, happy times we shared together last summer.

With admiration, love and gratitude, for the inspiration and the dreams she gave to all of us, we say goodbye to Jackie today.

May the flame she lit so long ago burn ever brighter here and always brighter in our hearts.

God bless you, friend, and farewell.

Bill Clinton

MR. CLINTON IS THE PRESIDENT OF THE UNITED STATES

At a party given by Prince Stanislas Radziwill and Jackie's sister Lee, which was attended by the British Prime Minister and members of British high society, the theater, and the press, Jackie again sparkled and was the true jewel of that gathering.

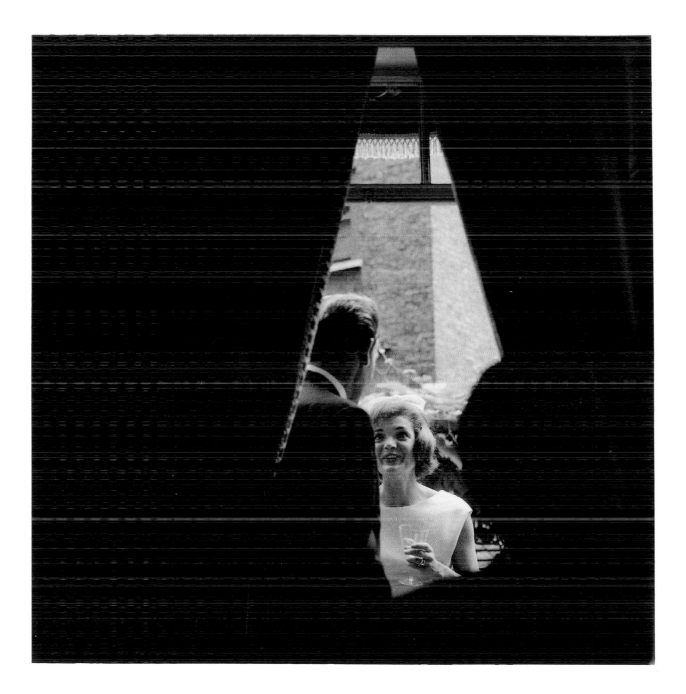

LONDON. JUNE 1961

121

L

Last summer, when we were on the upper deck on the boat at the Vineyard, waiting for President and Mrs. Clinton to arrive, Jackie turned to me and said: "Teddy, you go down and greet the President."

But I said: "Maurice (Tempelsman) is already there."

And Jackie answered: "Teddy, you do it. Maurice isn't running for re-election."

She was always there—for all our family—in her special way.

She was a blessing to us and to the nation, and a lesson to the world on how to do things right, how to be a mother, how to appreciate history, how to be courageous.

No one else looked like her, spoke like her, wrote like her, or was so original in the way she did things. No one we knew ever had a better sense of self.

Eight months before she married Jack, they went together to President Eisenhower's inaugural ball. Jackie said later that that's where they decided they like inaugurations.

No one ever gave more meaning to the title of First Lady. The nation's capital city looks as it does because of her. She saved Lafayette Square and Pennsylvania Avenue.

Jackie brought the greatest artists to the White House, and brought the arts to the center of national attention. Today, in large part because of her inspiration and vision, the arts are an abiding part of national policy.

President Kennedy took such delight in her brilliance and her spirit. At a White House dinner, he once leaned over and told the wife of the French ambassador, "Jackie speaks fluent French. But I only understand one out of every five words she says—and that word is DeGaulle."

And then, during those four endless days in 1963, she held us together as a family and a country. In large part because of her, we could grieve and

Lee Radziwill, Jackie's younger sister who lived in London at the time and her son Anthony on a visit to America during the summer of 1961.

HYANNIS PORT, MASSACHUSETTS. SUMMER 1961

then go on. She lifted us up and, in the doubt and darkness, she gave her fellow citizens back their pride as Americans. She was then 34 years old.

Afterward, as the eternal flame she lit flickered in the autumn of Arlington Cemetery, Jackie went on to do what she most wanted—to raise Caroline and John, and warm her family's life and that of all the Kennedys.

Robert Kennedy sustained her, and she helped make it possible for Bobby to continue. She kept Jack's memory alive, as he carried Jack's mission on.

Her two children turned out to be extraordinary, honest, unspoiled and with a character equal to hers. And she did it in the most trying of circumstances. They are her two miracles.

Her love for Caroline and John was deep and unqualified. She reveled in their accomplishments, she hurt with their sorrows, and she felt sheer joy and delight in spending time with them. At the mere mention of one of their names, Jackie's eyes would shine brighter and her smile would grow bigger.

She once said that if you "bungle raising your children, nothing else much matters in life." She didn't bungle. Once again, she showed us how to do the most important thing of all, and do it right.

When she went to work, Jackie became a respected professional in the world of publishing. And because of her, remarkable books came to life. She searched out new authors and ideas. She was interested in everything.

Her love of history became a devotion to historic preservation. You knew, when Jackie joined the cause to save a building in Manhattan, the bulldozers might as well turn around and go home.

She had a wonderful sense of humor—a way of focusing on someone with total attention—and a little girl delight in who they were and what they were saying. It was a gift of herself that she gave to others. And in spite of all her heartache and loss, she never faltered.

I often think of what she said about Jack in December after he died: "They made him a legend, when he would have preferred to be a man." Jackie would have preferred just to be herself, but the world insisted that she be a legend, too.

The five Kennedy women Joan, Jean Kennedy Smith, Eunice Kennedy Shriver, Jackie, and Ethel—on the porch of Ambassador Kennedy's home, known as 'The Big House'.

HYANNIS PORT, MASSACHUSETTS. AUGUST 1960

She never wanted public notice—in part, I think, because it brought back painful memories of an unbearable sorrow, endured in the glare of a million lights.

In all the years since then, her genuineness and depth of character continued to shine through the privacy, and reach people everywhere. Jackie was too young to be a widow in 1963, and too young to die now.

Her grandchildren were bringing new joy to her life, a joy that illuminated her face whenever you saw them together. Whether it was taking Rose and Tatiana for an ice cream cone, or taking a walk in Central Park with little Jack as she did last Sunday, she relished being Grand Jackie and showering her grandchildren with love.

At the end, she worried more about us than herself. She let her family and friends know she was thinking of them. How cherished were those wonderful notes in her distinctive hand on her powder-blue stationery!

In truth, she did everything she could—and more—for each of us.

She made a rare and noble contribution to the American spirit. But for us, most of all she was a magnificent wife, mother, grandmother, sister, aunt and friend.

She graced our history. And for those of us who knew and loved her— she graced our lives.

Edward M. Kennedy

MR. KENNEDY IS A UNITED STATES SENATOR FROM MASSACHUSETTS

The funeral procession for President Kennedy passes on the way to Arlington Cemetery.

WASHINGTON, D.C. NOVEMBER 23, 1963

127

Permissions